Your Growing Child

By the Editors of Time-Life Books

Alexandria, Virginia

Time-Life Books Inc.
is a wholly owned subsidiary of

Time Incorporated

FOUNDER: Henry R. Luce 1898-1967

Editor-in-Chief: Henry Anatole Grunwald
Chairman and Chief Executive Officer:
J. Richard Munro
President and Chief Operating Officer:
N. J. Nicholas Jr.
Chairman of the Executive Committee:
Ralph P. Davidson
Corporate Editor: Ray Cave
Executive Vice President, Books: Kelso F. Sutton
Vice President, Books: George Artandi

Time-Life Books Inc.

EDITOR: George Constable
Executive Editor: Ellen Phillips
Director of Design: Louis Klein
Director of Editorial Resources: Phyllis K. Wise
Editorial Board: Russell B. Adams Jr., Thomas H.
Flaherty, Lee Hassig, Donia Ann Steele, Rosalind
Stubenberg, Kit van Tulleken, Henry Woodhead
Director of Photography and Research:
John Conrad Weiser

PRESIDENT: Christopher T. Linen
Chief Operating Officer: John M. Fahey Jr.
Senior Vice Presidents: James L. Mercer,
Leopoldo Toralballa
Vice Presidents: Stephen L. Bair, Ralph J. Cuomo,
Neal Goff, Stephen L. Goldstein, Juanita T. James,
Hallett Johnson III, Robert H. Smith, Paul R. Stewart
Director of Production Services:
Robert J. Passantino

Library of Congress Cataloguing in
Publication Data
Your growing child.
    (Successful parenting)
    Bibliography: p.
    Includes index.
    1. Child development. I. Time-Life Books.
II. Series.
HQ767.9.Y68 1987   155.4'22   87-1912
ISBN 0-8094-5916-7
ISBN 0-8094-5917-5 (lib. bdg.)

Successful Parenting

SERIES DIRECTOR: Donia Ann Steele
Deputy Editor: Jim Hicks
Series Administrator: Norma E. Shaw
Editorial Staff for *Your Growing Child:*
Designer: Cynthia Richardson
Picture Editor: Jane Jordan
Text Editors: Dale M. Brown, Robert A. Doyle
Staff Writer: Charlotte Anker
Researchers: Charlotte Fullerton, Mark Moss
(principals), Rita Thievon Mullin,
Myrna Traylor-Herndon
Assistant Designer: Susan M. Gibas
Copy Coordinator: Marfé Ferguson
Picture Coordinator: Bradley Hower
Editorial Assistant: Jenester C. Lewis

Special Contributors: Amy Aldrich, George Daniels,
Dónal Kevin Gordon, Wendy Murphy (text);
Melva Holloman (research)

Editorial Operations
Copy Chief: Diane Ullius
Editorial Operations Manager: Caroline A. Boubin
Production: Celia Beattie
Library: Louise D. Forstall

Correspondents: Elisabeth Kraemer-Singh (Bonn);
Maria Vincenza Aloisi (Paris); Ann Natanson
(Rome).

First printing. Printed in U.S.A.

Published simultaneously in Canada.
School and library distribution by
Silver Burdett Company, Morristown,
New Jersey 07960.

TIME-LIFE is a trademark of Time
Incorporated U.S.A.

Other Publications:

FIX IT YOURSELF
FITNESS, HEALTH & NUTRITION
HEALTHY HOME COOKING
UNDERSTANDING COMPUTERS
LIBRARY OF NATIONS
THE ENCHANTED WORLD
THE KODAK LIBRARY OF CREATIVE PHOTOGRAPHY
GREAT MEALS IN MINUTES
THE CIVIL WAR
PLANET EARTH
COLLECTOR'S LIBRARY OF THE CIVIL WAR
THE EPIC OF FLIGHT
THE GOOD COOK
WORLD WAR II
HOME REPAIR AND IMPROVEMENT
THE OLD WEST

*For information on and a full description
of any of the Time-Life Books series listed
above, please write:*
Reader Information
Time-Life Books
541 North Fairbanks Court
Chicago, Illinois 60611

This volume is one of a series about raising children.

The Consultants

Dr. David Dickinson, who consulted on the language section of *Your Growing Child,* is assistant professor in reading and language arts at the Eliot-Pearson Department of Child Study at Tufts University. A former elementary school teacher, Dr. Dickinson has done considerable research and writing in the field of early childhood literacy and the interrelationships between spoken and written language. He is currently working on programs to foster positive attitudes toward reading among preschool children.

Dr. David L. Gallahue, professor and assistant dean at the Indiana University School of Health, Physical Education and Recreation, contributed to the material on developing physical skills and also to the posture essay in the first section of the book. Dr. Gallahue has created two films as well as numerous presentations, workshops and articles on the development of movement abilities in young children. Among the books Dr. Gallahue has written are *Understanding Motor Development in Children* and *Developmental Physical Education for Today's Children.*

Dr. Constance Keefer, consultant for the section on growth and responsibility, is a pediatrician, an instructor in pediatrics and director of a course in primary care jointly sponsored by the Harvard Medical School and the Harvard Community Health Plan of Boston. She is currently researching child-rearing theories of American parents. Dr. Keefer has recently completed work on a comparative study of American and Kenyan children with respect to early motor performance and mother-child interaction. She has also been a member of the guest faculty at the biannual conference of the National Center for Clinical Infant Programs, in Washington, D.C.

Dr. Jon F. Miller, who contributed to the material on language problems, has done a number of studies relating early language comprehension to other intellectual skills. He is currently professor of communicative disorders and coordinator of behavioral research at the Waisman Center on Mental Retardation and Human Development at the University of Wisconsin. Dr. Miller is also chairman of the Scientific Affairs Committee of the American Speech-Language-Hearing Association.

Dr. Vernon Thorpe Tolo, an expert on the bone and muscle structure of infants and children, helped develop the book's opening section on growth. He is associate professor of pediatrics and associate professor of orthopedic surgery at the Johns Hopkins University School of Medicine. Dr. Tolo also serves as attending orthopedic surgeon at the Children's Hospital of Baltimore and several other Baltimore-area medical centers. He has written and lectured widely on orthopedic issues concerning children and has been a featured speaker at state and national pediatric and orthopedic meetings.

Contents

3 Speech and Language   86

4 Learning Responsibility   108

How Children Grow

The gleeful expression radiating from the taller of the two children pictured at right tells us that growing up is great fun. Just eight months older than his smaller playmate, this four-year-old youngster has left behind the chubby contours of toddlerhood and now proudly boasts a frame that is lean and lithe.

Yet growing up involves much more than simply becoming taller and more slender, as you have already seen from the tremendous changes in your child during infancy. Little bones begin to harden, the first teeth emerge, baby muscles become firm, and organs and body systems start to mature. Throughout a child's preschool years, growth and development continue side by side, although at a somewhat less spectacular rate than in the first year of life.

All youngsters experience the same developmental patterns but they go through them in their own fashion, no two exactly alike. Your child will have inherited certain characteristics that will help determine his height, weight and body type. Yet there is much that you can do to assist nature and make sure that he achieves his fullest potential, by providing for him as supportive and healthy an environment as possible. A growing body needs proper nutrition, enough rest, plenty of fresh air and ample opportunity for exercise. And your child will want new challenges to test himself against as he develops greater physical strength and coordination.

Following Nature's Plan

The business of growing up is a continuous, orderly process, yet its rhythms can vary widely. During the years between the first and sixth birthdays, your child's growth may proceed like clockwork, or it may be puzzlingly uneven for any number of reasons — sex, heredity, glandular and emotional development, nutrition, climate, even the child's birth order within the family. Do not fret. Chances are that everything is moving along according to a special plan that nature designed just for that child.

These youngsters, all of them five years old, exemplify the uniqueness of growth. Each is of different height, weight and build. Gender, environment and ethnic characteristics account for some of the differences but not all. Every child grows at his or her own speed to fit an individual mold.

The words "growth" and "development" often are used interchangeably. But although closely related, physical growth and the development of skills are different processes. Growth can be regarded as quantitative change, development as qualitative change. To say that a child grows means that some part of her body increases in size or complexity. She adds inches or pounds; her bones become larger and stronger; her nervous system expands. Partly as a result of such physical changes, her skills and capabilities develop. Her larger size and stronger bones help her

to walk; her more mature nervous system allows her to think and learn. The interaction between your child's physical growth and the development of new skills can be likened to the back-and-forth exchange of strokes in a tennis game between two well-matched players. First your youngster progresses in physical or mental capacity; next she learns a skill that employs her new capability. Now her just-acquired skill encourages further growth; then she learns yet another related skill.

Patterns of growth Growth specialists have identified an overall formula for the postnatal changes in the human body: *2-3-4-5,* meaning that between birth and adulthood, an individual's head and neck dimensions will increase by two times, trunk by three times, arms by four times and legs by five times. The years between one and six involve enormous growth; most youngsters will have attained more than half their adult height by the first grade.

The growth and development that lead your youngster to this point proceed according to three principles, or sequences. The first is known as the cephalocaudal sequence, a name based on the Latin words for "head" and "tail." This principle decrees the growth of the head first, the trunk next and the legs last. At birth your child's head constitutes one quarter of her body length; at maturity, after the rest of her body has caught up, her head will represent only one eighth of her body length. The second principle of growth is called the proximodistal sequence (roughly, "near to far" in Latin), and it states that your youngster's body matures from the trunk outward to the extremities. For example, her central nervous system, consisting of the brain and spinal cord, will mature before her peripheral nervous system, the network of nerve fibers extending to all parts of the body.

The third principle, called differentiation, means that growth proceeds from the simple to the complex. The most dramatic illustration of this fascinating principle is the evolution of the individual from a single cell — the united egg and sperm — into a complex body possessing the specialized systems of the skin and nerves, muscles and bones, and the internal organs.

Different rates for different children Although growth has its consistent stages and definite patterns, it nevertheless proceeds at different rates in different children. One four-year-old may be tall and slender, while another still retains the short stature and pudgy cheeks of a toddler.

You will notice, too, that your child grows faster at some times than others. One month he may seem to outgrow his jeans and shirts virtually overnight. A short time later he may enter a period of slower growth. The growth of individual body parts is not always evenly paced, either. Your youngster's trunk may slim and lengthen before his face, or his feet may grow big before he loses his round, babyish tummy.

Putting knowledge into practice

Understanding the way your child's body grows can be of great help in caring for him. For example, one sturdy toddler had frequent ear infections that worried his parents until they learned that a young child's wide, horizontal Eustachian tubes give easy passage to both liquids and germs. As the child grows, these channels narrow and angle downward, and ear infections become less common. Once the parents understood why their child was susceptible to ear infections, they could guard against them by not allowing him to fall asleep while drinking a bottle of warm milk, a practice that can easily result in the transmittal of bacteria from the throat to the ears.

A basic understanding of the ways children grow will also allow you to offer the sorts of stimulation and challenge that match their physical abilities. And a knowledge of nature's scheme will enable you to relax and appreciate your youngster's progress, confident that you will notice any significant problems in his growth.

The influence of growth on self-esteem

For a young child, the physical side of life dominates, and the continuous physical process of growing up has an impact on the whole person, particularly on her emerging sense of self-esteem. As a toddler she will be aware of her own small size in relation to adults, and this may make her somewhat shy. But as she grows and develops, gaining both stature and competence, she will acquire self-confidence as well, gradually shedding her early timidity. The five-year-old who is pleased with her own size and shape and growth progress is likely to enjoy a similarly favorable opinion of herself in other areas. For that reason, it is always a good idea to emphasize your own satisfaction with your child's stature and pace of growth.

Growth and sleep

Your child's pattern of sleep is subject to change and development just as her body is. As an infant she spent a great deal of her sleeptime — as much as 50 percent — in what is called active sleep, similar to the dreaming sleep stage of older children and adults. Although experts have no way of knowing whether babies actually dream, active sleep of this type does exercise the brain, possibly helping it to mature.

In older children and adults, this stimulating, dream-filled

sleep is called rapid eye movement (REM) sleep. Like the infant's active sleep, it is characterized by eye movements, visible beneath the lids, and slight body twitches. As she grows, your child will spend progressively less time in active, or REM, sleep, until at the age of five only about 20 percent of her sleeping hours will be in the REM phase; the rest will be in deep, quiet slumber.

The total time your child spends sleeping changes as well. Although the connection between sleep and growth is not entirely clear, children seem to sleep proportionately more during periods of rapid physical change than during lulls in growth, and the overall need for sleep declines as a child grows older. For example, growth begins to slacken just a bit after the age of one and so does the amount of time spent in slumber. The typical one-year-old naps for about one hour in the morning and two in the afternoon and sleeps through the night for about 12 hours.

Phasing Out Naptime

66 Now that Brian is two and a half, I've found that if he takes a nap during the day he will be bouncing off the walls at midnight, wide awake. So I decided to wean him from his nap — and it's hard work, because around five o'clock he's ready to drop. It's a difficult hour because he's hungry and tired, and I need to be fixing dinner. If I give him projects that need concentration, such as block and puzzle play, he gets frustrated easily. If he watches TV, he falls asleep. The best activity during that time seems to be painting: It keeps him awake but also gives him some relaxation. 99

66 Justin and Samantha — who are only one year apart — were cranky when they gave up their naps. And I didn't like giving up my pick-me-up period. But the transition only lasted about a month, and then we were all set in a new schedule where quiet time replaced their regular naptime. I began to see the advantage of no naps — I could plan outings at any time of the day. 99

66 I used to lie down with Luke and nurse him after lunch and expect him to go to sleep. At two he began to get right up with me and I would say, 'Oh well, I guess that was the nap.' He still really needed some rest and if he fell asleep at five, I could expect to stay up until midnight with him. I tried to go with the flow and let him outgrow the need for the late afternoon nap. My attitude was, 'What the heck, I'll just enjoy him whenever he is awake.' 99

66 We used to call Chlöe the 'sleepless wonder.' I desperately needed the time, and she clearly needed the rest, but she fought her naps. Whenever I put her down she would come up with clever requests: 'Oh Mommy, I forgot to kiss you,' 'I need to tell you something; I want to whisper it in your ear,' 'Mommy you are so pretty, let me look at your face.' Her three-year-old manipulations seemed so ingenious, I couldn't resist going to her. As a stress-management expert, I thought I knew all the tricks on how to cope with a sleepless wonder, but after a while I decided it was pointless to keep saying, 'Go to sleep.' So we skipped naps from then on. 99

66 Our naptime routine evolved out of going to the pool during the summer. Peter and David would fall asleep coming home in the car, I would put them in their beds and then I could count on their sleeping for two hours. When the pool closed and I wasn't driving every afternoon, they wouldn't take their naps. Instead of fighting with them I said, 'Okay, let's get in the car and take a little drive.' They would fall asleep, I would carry them back into the house, and they would nap. That worked for a full year until Peter turned four and a half. Now he is on to me. In fact, both of the boys are on to me now, but David still falls asleep in the car. 99

66 'Can I get up yet?' I would hear this question after Robbie had only been down for one minute. I felt it was okay for him to be awake as long as he stayed quietly in his room for at least 45 minutes. We made that the rule, and Robbie did not protest: He liked playing alone quietly with his toys. He just did not want to have to go to sleep. 99

At two, as the growth rate tapers off further, most children give up a nap — usually the morning one. Your child will probably benefit from her afternoon nap until she is three or older; after that, her nightly slumber should be enough. Abandoning the afternoon nap can be a big transition; base your handling of it on your child's special needs and personality (page 12).

The average preschooler sleeps 11 to 11 and a half hours each night, but there is a wide range in the amount of sleep different children need. One child may nod off just after dinner, while another of the same age is perky well into the evening. With sleep, as with all other aspects of child rearing, you should take care to observe and respect your child's individual rhythms. ⁛

Influences on Growth

From the moment of birth, your child exhibits his own distinct physical features and personality, determined by the genetic material of egg and sperm cells that united at conception. As he grows, his height and weight, the curve of his jaw and the timbre of his voice are all to a large extent already decided.

Yet your youngster also enters the world as an open, flexible being whose growth will be shaped by many environmental influences. Some of these, such as nutrition, exercise and health care, can be controlled by parents. Ultimately, it is the interplay of nature's gifts and nurture's assistance that forms the whole person. Your goal as a parent is to help your youngster achieve his potential without pushing him to meet standards beyond the limits of his genetic make-up.

The role of genes
By and large, you can expect your child to be a lot like you. Offspring of tall, muscular parents are likely to be larger and more muscular than children with petite parents. Of course, there are exceptions caused either by environmental influences such as improved nutrition or by genes that have lain hidden for a generation or more, resulting in the husky young football player whose parents are both slight, or a short child who has tall parents. But in general, height, weight and physique reflect the parents' builds. How quickly your youngster grows and matures, too, will approximate your own rate of growth as a child. If your baby cuts his first tooth unexpectedly early, you may find by asking your own parents that he is simply following in your path.

Such characteristics and patterns are passed from generation to generation by means of genetic material — special molecules that exist at the center of all the cells of the body. This same genetic material also controls the broad categories of gender and race, which, in themselves, strongly influence a child's size and rate of maturation. If your young child is a boy, he is likely to be just a bit heavier and taller than most girls his age, and he probably will keep his lead throughout early childhood. Young girls, on the other hand, tend to acquire sturdy bones and their first permanent teeth somewhat in advance of boys.

The effect of hormones
Hormones, internal secretions produced by endocrine glands in the head and trunk, affect a number of the body's most basic functions, among them growth and development. The hormones produced in the pituitary and thyroid glands play a particularly significant role in prompting a young child's growth.

The special hormone that controls overall growth is produced in the pituitary, an oval-shaped gland located at the base of the

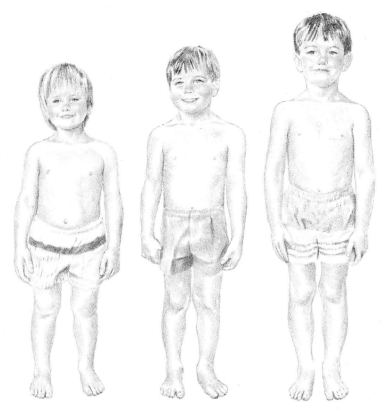

During the preschool years children lose their babyish figures and begin to assume the physiques they will carry as adults. These five-year-olds illustrate the three main types of physique, as seen in hips, shoulders and limbs. The lad at far right will likely turn out tall and slender, the boy at near right broad and stocky, while the one at center will be of average musculature in build.

brain. By promoting cell division, specifically at bone ends, this so-called human-growth hormone regulates the increases in a youngster's height, one of the most visible measures of his growth. A child who is extremely short for his age may have too little growth hormone and should be tested; the hormone can be given by injection when the body is not producing enough.

The thyroid, a butterfly-shaped gland in the throat, manufactures thyroxine, which helps a child's bones, teeth and brain to mature. It, too, can affect growth: Abnormally short stature is sometimes due to a deficiency of thyroxine. In such cases, therapy with doses of the hormone will encourage a return to normal growth. Thyroxine also plays a key role in controlling metabolism — the rate at which the body processes food — and therefore influences a child's weight.

The brain's growth center Just above the pituitary gland is a segment of the brain called the hypothalamus, which stimulates the pituitary into action. In recent years researchers have suggested that this almond-size bit of tissue functions to monitor growth, supervising how fast and toward what target your child advances. When progress slows for some reason — illness, perhaps — the hypothalamus registers the deviation. Once your youngster regains good health, the hypothalamus speeds up his growth until he is back on course. The process can be likened to an airplane following a flight plan toward a destination. If all goes well, the plane travels along the preestablished route and arrives at its destination on time. Should the plane encounter bad weather, its progress may be slowed, in which case the pilot may fly at a greater speed or even take a shortcut. Similarly, when the child whose progress is interrupted resumes growth, it is often at a faster pace and along a shorter path to his internally preset goal.

How environment affects growth

Many features of a youngster's environment help determine her rate of growth and whether she fulfills the promise of her genes. Even conditions before birth have an impact: A child with the genetic predisposition to be large who was cramped during the last few weeks of gestation will grow more rapidly than an infant whose growth was not constricted. Conversely, an infant who was large at birth but genetically predisposed to be a small person may grow relatively slowly for a while. These effects may last until about the age of two, when the growth rate becomes more like the average for the youngster's age.

The season of the year affects growth, too, possibly due to varying amounts of sunlight that the child receives. For whatever reason, spring and summer usually prompt an acceleration in upward growth. A similar seasonal effect applies to weight, which tends to increase more rapidly in autumn and winter. When evaluating your child's growth, be sure to take into account all the spurts and lapses that occur over the entire year: The four-year-old who seemed a bit spindly over the summer may put on some needed bulk once the days shorten and cooler weather sets in.

Naturally, you cannot control how much room your baby has to grow in during the last few weeks of gestation. And there is not much you can do about the season. There is, however, quite a lot you can accomplish in other areas of your child's environment. Adequate nutrition and good health care are very important. Poor nutrition and illness can both temporarily delay a child's normal progress. Emotional health is as critical as physical health, for stress and anxiety often result in loss of sleep and appetite, jeopardizing growth processes. Severe distress may upset a child's metabolism and hormonal balance as well, further affecting growth.

One way to promote good health is through physical activity. Exercise encourages the development of bone tissue and strengthens muscles. It also contributes to a youngster's emotional well-being and may even stimulate the pituitary's secretion of growth hormone.

Nutrients for Healthy Growing

Nutrients — the chemical substances obtained through food and drink — are the essential fuels of life. The body uses these substances in numerous ways — to supply energy, build and maintain body cells, and regulate the body processes. There are about 50 essential nutrients, grouped into six categories: proteins, carbohydrates, fats, vitamins, minerals and water.

Water is the most important nutrient of all because without it, life would soon end. Vitamins and minerals are required only in relatively small quantities each day. The 13 vitamins are organic substances that help the body process all nutrients and form hormones, blood cells and tissue. The important minerals are 17 in number; they are inorganic substances that help build strong bones and perform other critical functions.

All 50 nutrients, along with sunlight as a source of vitamins, are particularly important for a growing child. If your child's diet contains plenty of the 10 leading nutrients described below, it is most likely also providing enough of the remaining nutrients for proper growth and glowing good health.

Protein *is critically important to growth. It supplies energy, helps build, repair and replace tissue, makes infection-fighting antibodies and regulates the body's metabolism — the process of converting nutrients to energy or cell material.*
SOURCES: meat, poultry, fish and shellfish, eggs, dairy products, legumes, nuts.

Carbohydrates *in their digested form make glucose, a sugar that is the body's primary energy source. Carbohydrates supply energy for the brain, are required for nerve tissue and the liver to function, and in dietary fiber form, aid elimination.*
SOURCES: whole grains, brown rice, legumes, potatoes, corn, fruit, nuts.

Fats, *an essential part of diet, provide twice the energy of proteins or carbohydrates ounce for ounce. Fats cushion vital organs, provide and carry vitamins, and supply needed fatty acids. But animal fats, which contain cholesterol, can be harmful when consumed to excess.*
SOURCES: meat, nuts, margarine, vegetable oils.

Vitamin A *promotes healthy skin, night and color vision, strong bones and teeth, and growth and repair of all body cells, especially the mucous membranes of the eyelids, eyes, nose, mouth and digestive tract.*
SOURCES: liver, dairy products, green and yellow vegetables, such fruits as cantaloupes and peaches.

Vitamin C *maintains healthy gums, teeth and bones, promotes healing and resistance to infection, and enhances the body's use of iron. It also maintains the elasticity of blood vessels, thus reducing bruises.*
SOURCES: citrus fruits, cabbage, green peppers, tomatoes, potatoes, dark green vegetables.

Vitamin B₁ (thiamin) *breaks down carbohydrates for energy, regulates the nervous system, stimulates appetite and helps maintain the digestive system and heart. Thiamin also enhances tissue growth and repair.*
SOURCES: lean pork, fish, shellfish, dairy products, whole- or enriched-grain products, nuts, legumes.

Vitamin B₃ (niacin) *works with thiamin and riboflavin to help the body produce energy and is important for appetite, good digestion, healthy skin and nerves.*
SOURCES: liver, meat, poultry, fish, eggs, whole- or enriched-grain products, nuts, potatoes, tomatoes, mushrooms, legumes, dark green vegetables.

Vitamin B₂ (riboflavin), *like thiamin, helps release energy from carbohydrates. It also breaks down fats and proteins, promotes healthy skin and vision, and aids in maintaining the body's mucous membranes.*
SOURCES: liver, dairy products, meat, whole-grain or enriched-grain products, legumes, leafy greens.

Calcium *is the body's most abundant material, next to water. It gives strength to bones and teeth, and permits proper muscle contraction, nerve transmission, blood-clotting and the absorption of certain B vitamins.*
SOURCES: dairy products, fish, citrus fruits, nuts, legumes, leafy dark green vegetables.

Iron *aids the formation of hemoglobin in the red blood cells, carries oxygen to and carbon dioxide from the cells, helps develop new muscle tissue, promotes resistance to infection and prevents nutritional anemia.*
SOURCES: liver, meat, dried fruit, whole-grain or enriched-grain products, potatoes, legumes, leafy greens.

Nutrients and diet   Of the many environmental factors that influence growth, nutrition is the most basic. The box on page 16 identifies the nutrients most essential to a young child and specifies their roles in healthy growth.

You may be surprised to find water mentioned as a class of nutrients. Yet the body's need for water is second only to its demand for oxygen. Water makes up 85 percent of a newborn's body, compared to 66 percent in an adult. It serves as a building nutrient and transports other nutrients to the cells; it dissolves wastes and carries them away, and it acts as a primary regulator of your child's body temperature. Each day a youngster will urinate or perspire away about 65 percent of the water needed to maintain her body. And it all must be replaced, though not necessarily by drinking huge amounts. Every food contains water: Fruits and vegetables are 80 to 95 percent water; meat, poultry and fish are 50 to 75 percent water; milk is 87 percent water. A balanced diet of food and drink will keep your youngster properly hydrated.

For most children a varied diet of simple, wholesome foods will also supply enough of the 50 or so other nutrients required for good health. And nutritionists point out that the stress should be on the quality of the food a youngster is fed, rather than its quantity. Some parents worry unnecessarily that their children are not getting sufficient nourishment and, as a result, allow or even encourage them to overeat. But when a young child eats too much — or eats foods excessively high in calories — she may acquire an overabundance of fat-containing cells. Because all the fat-containing cells a person accumulates during gestation and early childhood stay with her throughout the adult years, a child who gains a greater than normal number of fat cells in childhood often finds it difficult to remain slim as an adult.

Fortunately, childhood is a time when it is relatively easy to reverse a trend toward overweight. The growth curves on the following pages show the normal rates at which height and weight increase in children from birth to the age of six. If your child's weight curve suddenly shoots upward, out of kilter with the average, you may want to consider an adjustment in her diet, in consultation with her pediatrician.

The growth curves also are helpful when your youngster goes through a period of light eating that concerns you. During such times — which can be triggered by illness or even by intense interest in physical activity and exploration — growth may slow or stop altogether. But once your child begins eating normally again, she will almost certainly make up for it. ❖

Tracking Your Child's Progress in Height and Weight

The rate at which children grow taller and gain weight is an important indication of their general health and should be monitored with care. At every well-child checkup, your pediatrician will measure your youngster's height and weight and will probably compare those figures with graphs like the ones appearing here and on the following two pages. You can do the same at home if you wish to keep your own records. The graphs can tell you how your child relates in these two areas to a large sampling of other American children at the same age.

Naturally, the graphs show variations between girls and boys and between individual children of the same sex. The curved lines represent divisions between percentile groups, numbered in ascending order. On the graphs below, for instance, the 10th percentile line separates the shortest 10 percent of the children measured in the surveys that produced the graphs from the taller 90 percent. And

Boys' Heights

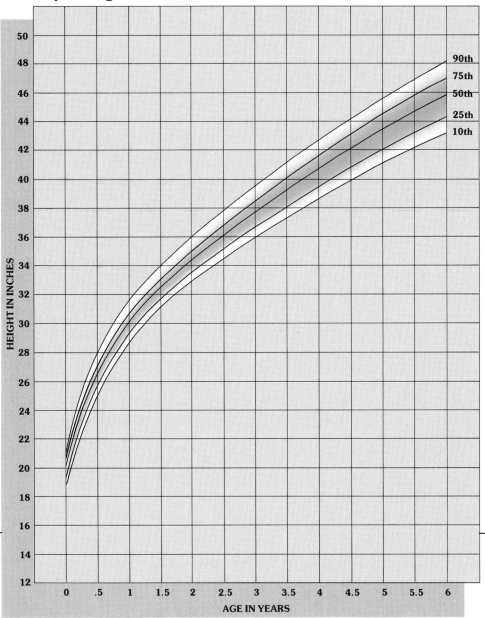

Find your child's height along the vertical scale at the left of the appropriate graph — the one at left for a boy and the graph opposite for a girl. Then locate your youngster's age along the horizontal scale across the bottom, using the six-month interval marks as a guide. Trace straight lines from both points to where they cross on the graph. Mark the spot, then follow the curved line nearest to that intersection to its end, to see what percentile it represents. If the mark you made is close to the 25th percentile line, for example, you will know that about 25 percent of youngsters of that age and sex are shorter than your child, and 75 percent are taller.

Mark your child's height on the graph periodically. The marks will not form a smooth curve exactly matching the percentile lines, but if your child is growing normally, they should roughly follow the curve of those lines. If instead the marks indicate a continued, significant change in percentile ranking, your youngster may have a growth problem — a rare situation — and you should consult his pediatrician.

children whose heights were plotted above the 90th percentile line were in the tallest 10 percent of those measured. As the shaded areas indicate, the largest concentrations of measurements fall in the middle range, along both sides of the 50th percentile that divides the taller half of the children from the shorter half.

Of course, children do not grow as evenly as the graphs make it appear. The bumpier curves produced by simply averaging the measurements have been smoothed out by computer — much as a radio signal can be cleaned of random noise and static to leave a clear tone. The smoothing of the curves makes it easier to

assess the meaning of an individual child's growth pattern.

To obtain figures comparable to those from which the graphs were compiled, measure a child younger than two years old while she is lying on her back and measure an older child in a standing position. To measure a child who is lying down,

Girls' Heights

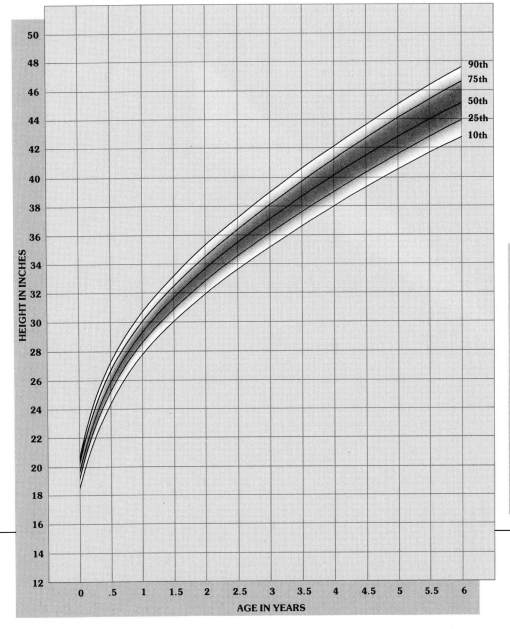

HEIGHT IN INCHES

90th
75th
50th
25th
10th

AGE IN YEARS

Predicting Adult Height

You can forecast your youngster's eventual adult height with reasonable accuracy by applying one of the following formulas.

Boys:

Height at two years x 2

————— = adult height

Girls:

Height at 1.5 years x 2

————— = adult height

position her on a large sheet of paper with her feet against a vertical surface, such as the wall if you are measuring her on the floor, or a heavy box if you are measuring her on a table. See that her legs are as straight as possible without forcing them. Use a book or other right-angled object *(page 31)* to take the measurement.

Children in the surveys were weighed on balance scales like those used by doctors; if you are using a spring scale, make sure it is accurate. Your youngster should be naked or dressed in underpants or other very light clothing while being weighed. You can wrap an infant in a blanket for weighing, then weigh the blan-

ket separately and subtract that figure from the first reading.

A look at the graphs will show you that all children grow according to much the same pattern. The rate of growth — which is actually greatest during the first four months in the womb — is relatively high at birth, but eases off from then until

Boys' Weights

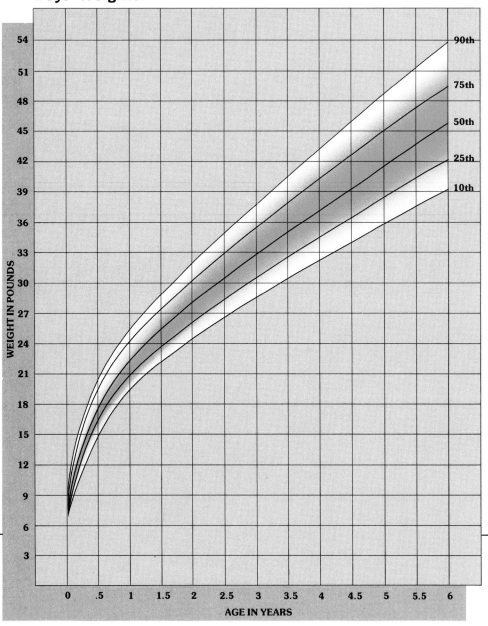

Find your child's weight on the vertical line at the left of the appropriate graph and the child's age along the horizontal scale at the bottom. Then use the same method described in the height graph caption on page 18 to determine the youngster's percentile position. Weigh your child and mark the graph at regular intervals to see if weight change roughly keeps pace with the percentile curve. A significant rise in percentile ranking over a period of time might mean a child is putting on more weight than needed; a significant fall in ranking could mean he is not gaining enough.

Compare your youngster's weight percentile with his height percentile. A large difference between the two could be a sign of a problem. If a youngster ranks in a low height percentile and a high weight percentile, for instance, he may be unhealthily overweight. A weight percentile substantially lower than height percentile could mean the child is ill or undernourished.

about the fourth year, at which point it stabilizes. (It will spurt ahead again to a faster rate of increase at adolescence, a period not shown on these graphs.)

The average child will add almost 10 inches in height the first year, four to five inches the second year, three to four inches during each of the third and fourth years, and two to three inches a year from then until puberty. Weight more than doubles in the first year and after that increases by about five pounds a year until the child reaches puberty.

A number of factors, including heredity and conditions for the fetus in the womb, determine the height and weight percentile rankings of a newborn child. As youngsters grow after birth, the important thing is for them to maintain their positions relative to their peers. If children remain on or near the curves for their particular percentiles, especially in height, parents can rest assured that their offspring are growing normally. ❖

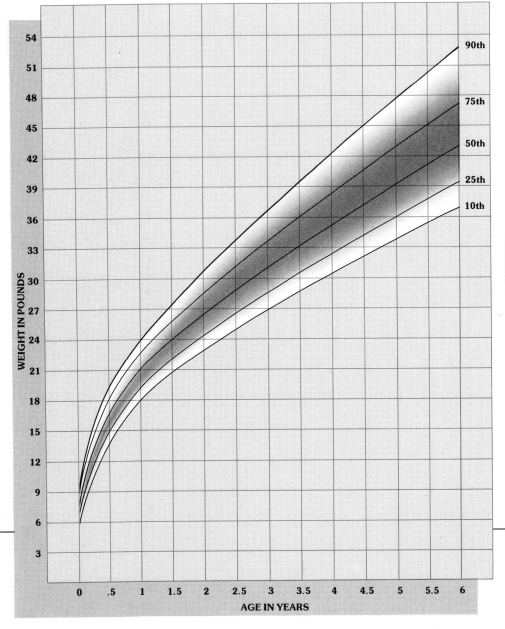

Girls' Weights

(y-axis: WEIGHT IN POUNDS — 3, 6, 9, 12, 15, 18, 21, 24, 27, 30, 33, 36, 39, 42, 45, 48, 51, 54)
(x-axis: AGE IN YEARS — 0, .5, 1, 1.5, 2, 2.5, 3, 3.5, 4, 4.5, 5, 5.5, 6)
(curves labeled: 90th, 75th, 50th, 25th, 10th)

Predicting Adult Weight

Although the weight of an adult can fluctuate greatly over time, you can obtain a rough forecast of your child's adult weight by using the following formulas.

Boys:

$$\frac{\text{Weight at two years} \times 5}{} = \text{adult weight}$$

Girls:

$$\frac{\text{Weight at 1.5 years} \times 5}{} = \text{adult weight}$$

Patterns of Physical Change

Many children expect to see themselves change overnight. One young lady looked in the mirror the moment she awakened on her sixth birthday, eager to see how different she looked now that she was a year older. Of course she was disappointed, for her reflection looked just as it had the day before. But when her parents sat her down in front of the family photo album, she could see how tremendously she had changed, if not exactly overnight, then in the space of just a few years.

Nearly every system and body part grows and develops between your child's first and sixth birthdays. The most evident growth is, of course, her transformation from a short, chubby toddler to a sturdy, well-built youngster. Between the ages of one and six, she adds about 16 inches to her height, and her body proportions shift significantly. As a baby, she has a large head and trunk and rather stubby arms and legs. During the toddler and preschool years, her arms and legs grow quickly while her head and trunk grow relatively slowly. These changes — along with her added height — are responsible for your youngster's new, more grown-up appearance.

During this time, her bones become larger as well as longer, a full set of primary teeth emerge, and internal organs mature. Of great importance is the rapid growth and development of her brain and nervous system, enabling her to perform an increasingly wide range of tasks.

How the brain and nervous system grow

Even though the brain is quite sizable at birth in relation to the rest of the body, a newborn baby is relatively helpless. It is only as your child's brain and nervous system grow and mature that he increases his ability to move about, think and register the many impressions received through the senses.

To understand the growth that takes place in your youngster's brain and nervous system, you need to know something of his anatomy. The body's overall controlling mechanism is made up of three parts: the brain and the spinal cord, which compose the body's central nervous system, and the peripheral nervous system, composed of the fibers that fan out from the brain and spinal cord to all parts of the body.

Brain tissue is composed of masses of neurons — nerve cells that transmit and receive messages — and support cells that nourish the delicate neurons. Each movement the body makes originates in messages, or impulses, generated by neurons. The impulses travel along slender branches that radiate from a neuron's core and extend through the rest of the body. It is these branches that form the bundles of fibers commonly called nerves. Most nerves originate in the brain; some originate at neurons along the spinal cord. As a youngster grows, many of his nerves become sheathed in myelin, which is a white, fatty substance that helps channel impulses along the nerves in much the same way that insulation keeps an electric current running smoothly along a wire.

At birth or shortly afterward, a child's brain has all the neurons it will ever have, but the network of fibers that branches from them is sparse, limiting the transmission of messages. The neurons also lack support cells and the insulating myelin that expe-

The bodies of these two sisters, one four years old and the other 18 months, show how body proportions change as children grow older. The toddler still has short legs and a round, babyish tummy, while her big sister has grown slender and agile-looking.

dites the impulses in their travels. Over the next few years, the neurons will sprout many thousands of connecting fibers, and new tissue — support cells and myelin sheathing along nerves — will grow. As a result, the brain will operate more efficiently, and the child will develop new capabilities.

To a large extent, the order in which the brain grows and matures governs the order in which a child masters his body and acquires skills. In the area of the brain that controls movement, for example, those neurons in charge of the arms and upper body mature earlier than those in charge of the legs. As a result, the child controls his arms before he walks.

Much of the brain's growth takes place in the first two years of life. You will notice that around his second birthday, your child's motor control is greatly improved. He also begins to talk, demonstrating the brain's greatly enhanced capabilities. At three, most children begin to use one hand more frequently than the other — a further sign of the brain's newly acquired sophistication. By the age of six, although the child's body is still small, his brain is nearly adult-size, and the support cells, connecting fibers and myelin sheathing are largely in place.

Sensory perception Some of the nerves of the peripheral nervous system are dedicated to the body's five senses: sight, hearing, touch, taste and smell. They channel information from the sense organs to the brain, where it is analyzed and interpreted. The eye, for instance, transforms light waves bouncing off an object into nerve impulses that travel to the brain, which then creates a picture of the object.

The tissue of the eyes — as well as that of the ears, nose, mouth and skin — contains special receptors that pick up sensory impressions and pass them on to the peripheral nerves. How well a child sees and hears, what she is able to smell and taste, and her sensitivity to touch all depend, in part, on the condition of these receptors. In general, children are born with their receptors in good working order, although some organs and nerves will grow and mature.

A child's perceptions also depend on the development of tissue in the part of the brain responsible for registering each sense and on the brain's capacity to make associations. An infant can smell fairly well, for example. But she has few associations with the various odors she sniffs and thus does not use her sense of smell very effectively. If she detected smoke, it would not mean fire to her. Gradually, your youngster will develop associations with smells and with the other sensations she experiences, a

lifelong process that is most intense during early childhood
when all the world lies waiting to be explored.

Although touch is for a time the most important of a newborn's
five senses — the primary form of communication between the
baby and his parents — a child's sense of touch is not fully developed at birth. His skin will have thousands of receptors to pick
up messages about temperature, pressure, texture and pain. He
certainly will feel pain, although he will be unable to pinpoint its
source, but he will not have the delicacy of touch to tell him
whether a blanket is rough or smooth. His sense of fine touch
will appear as the nerves myelinate, growing the white, fatty
coating that helps them transmit messages. Since according to
nature's formula, the nerves of the head and face myelinate before those of the extremities, a baby will constantly put things
into his mouth; one reason for this is that it helps him to feel
them more accurately. As your youngster moves into the toddler
years and the nerves in his arms and hands develop more completely, he will be able to satisfy his curiosity about the feel of an
object without immediately mouthing it.

Sight   Your toddler sees things a bit differently than you do, because
her short eyeballs cause close-up objects to appear out of focus.
This farsightedness will lessen during the next few years, as her
eyeballs grow. When the child is six, her visual acuity — the

ability to see objects sharply, whether near or far — should be at its peak. She also will be able to detect subtle gradations in color, distinguishing a pale blue shirt, for instance, from a pale turquoise one — something she could not do as an infant. A child's depth perception improves with age, too, as the brain is better able to coordinate eye muscles and combine images from each eye smoothly. First-graders usually have accurate depth perception, although this type of vision may improve still further in later years, possibly due to practice.

Hearing Unlike the senses of touch and vision, the hearing mechanism of the ear is fully developed at birth. But although babies and young children hear quite well, their ability to use the sense of hearing effectively increases as the brain matures. Sometime around the age of nine months, a child will turn her head for the first time when you say her name, and her alert gaze will seem to say, "That's me." At this exciting moment, not only is your youngster's ear transmitting a sound clearly to her brain, but her brain has matured enough to recognize the sound and assign a meaning to it.

During the next five years, your child's ability to relate sounds to meanings expands enormously, due partly to simple experience and partly to the brain's capabilities. A preschooler is increasingly able to hear subtle distinctions in sound, so that she speaks more clearly and, eventually, learns to read.

Taste and smell Tastes and odors often occur together — particularly in foods — but the body transmits the two impressions along different pathways to the brain. Taste buds — sensory receptors on the tongue — pick up flavors, while soft tissue inside the nose contains millions of smell receptors.

Even as an infant, a child is well-equipped to taste the full range of flavors and to sniff all the odors the world has to offer. What is missing is a range of associations with various tastes and scents — and therefore any well-defined preferences. After all, as a small baby, your child had a basic diet limited to milk for many months. As his experience with foods widens, he will remember flavors and develop preferences. He also will employ vision to guide him in his choices, imagining a pleasant or unpleasant taste by the way a food appears. If he previously ate something he did not like that looked similar to spinach, for example, he may well refuse spinach the very first time you offer it to him.

While children do have built-in preferences for sweet flavors and a natural aversion to foods that are bitter, other taste likes and dislikes are largely acquired. And preferences for smells are gradually learned: Whether your youngster's nose twitches happily at the smell of flowers or of zoo animals will depend up to a point on how he sees others around him reacting.

Skin
The largest of the organs, skin is the body's first line of defense against infection. It consists of two tightly connected layers of protective tissue. The thin outer layer, or epidermis, contains both dead cells that are continually sloughed off and a lining of new, living cells that multiply constantly, rising to the surface to replace those cast away. Beneath the epidermis is the dermis, a much thicker layer that contains blood vessels, nerve endings and glands.

Even a baby's velvety-smooth skin has this complex structure. It is, however, more fragile than mature skin, and it is less able to keep moisture in the body and infectious organisms out. An infant's skin is also vulnerable to surface irritations such as rashes and eczema.

Your youngster's skin will mature during his toddler years, becoming thicker, stronger and consequently better able to withstand troublesome germs. It will also be more resistant to irritation than when he was an infant. However, his skin at this age will still have a tendency to become dry, since the sebaceous glands, which produce a moisturizing substance, are generally inactive in young children.

Hair and nails
A child inherits from his parents the eventual characteristics of his hair — its color, thickness and curliness. But almost all children are born with a temporary head of short, soft, baby-fine hair that may not resemble their eventual hair color and consistency at all. As a child grows, his baby hair is gradually shed and replaced by coarser and darker hair. The mature shade and texture are not established until the age of two years or later, and even after that a child's hair often turns darker.

Shafts of hair grow from individual follicles that are embedded in the scalp. The growth occurs at the rate of about one-half inch per month, in a cyclical pattern: Each hair has a growth phase followed by a rest phase in which the shaft gradually loosens, eventually to be pushed out by a new hair growing in its place. In this normal process of growth and replacement, a child may lose up to 100 hairs per day. How thickly your youngster's hair grows depends upon the number of follicles that his scalp contains; the follicles are established before birth, and new ones are not formed later in life. This density, as well as the thickness of individual hairs, is determined by heredity.

Toenails and fingernails, present from birth, are an outgrowth of the skin similar to hair in composition and growth patterns. Delicate and thin in an infant, the nails gradually become thicker and harder as the child grows.

The digestive and urinary systems

During the preschool years your child's stomach capacity will steadily increase, although usually not sufficiently to carry her from one meal to the next. Many toddlers and preschoolers need nourishing between-meal snacks to keep up their blood sugar during these years of rapid growth. As your child grows, she will begin to digest solids more efficiently than she did as a baby, because her glands will produce greater amounts of saliva and other secretions that aid in breaking down food. Moreover, food now moves more slowly through the digestive tract, because the stomach is larger and the intestines are longer; as a result, diarrhea is less likely.

Perhaps the most welcome sign of internal growth and development is your toddler's emerging ability to control her bladder and bowels. For most children, this becomes physically possible as they approach their second birthday or shortly afterward. By this time, your child will be conscious of her body's functions and will have sufficient control over the necessary muscles. Consciousness comes about as the nerves leading to the bowel and bladder become better able to transmit messages to the brain; control grows as the child's muscles strengthen and come under the brain's supervision.

Your toddler's urinary control is helped along by her bladder's increasing size. Naturally, a larger bladder means that she will not have to empty it as frequently. Since children often neglect going to the toilet simply because they are too busy playing, this greater capacity automatically serves to reduce the number of toileting accidents.

Circulatory and respiratory systems

A baby weighs about seven pounds, and a five-year-old tips the scales at around 40 pounds, so it is not surprising that the heart — which must pump blood to the farthest reaches of the growing body — quadruples in weight during these years. The circulatory system matures, too, although in a more subtle way. In the first few years of life, the capillaries — the network of tiny blood vessels near the skin's surface — become more responsive to changes in environmental temperature. They widen to allow the blood to cool when the child gets too warm, and they narrow to keep the blood warm when cool air causes a chill.

When the Primary Teeth Appear

This chart shows the most common order and the likeliest times for the emergence of the primary, or baby, teeth. Usually the process is well under way by a child's first birthday and continues until all 20 teeth are in place, just before he turns three. For each stage, the teeth that are shaded in the chart are new arrivals; those that are white are the ones that have appeared previously. The timing varies widely from one child to another, but the teeth probably will appear in a sequence that is very similar to that shown here.

At birth all of these baby teeth are already in place in the child's jawbone, although all are probably hidden below his gums. The crown, or upper part, of each tooth begins to form while the child is still in the womb. The root, which holds the tooth in position, does not form fully until after birth. During the three-year period when the child's primary teeth are appearing, the crowns of his 32 permanent teeth are already forming beneath them in his jaw, although this second set of teeth will not begin to emerge until after he is about six years old.

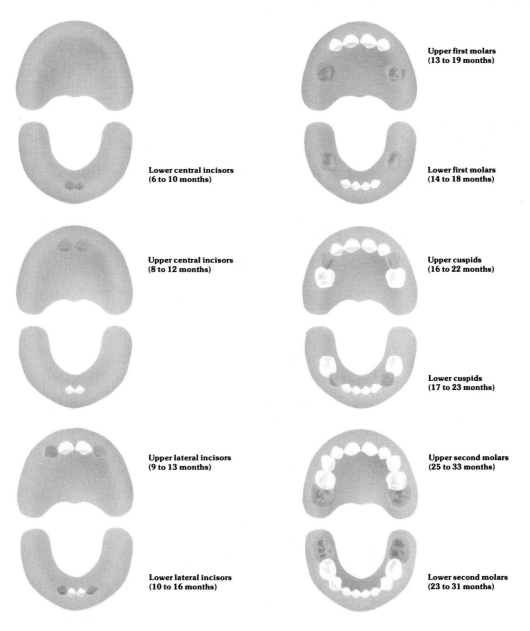

Lower central incisors
(6 to 10 months)

Upper central incisors
(8 to 12 months)

Upper lateral incisors
(9 to 13 months)

Lower lateral incisors
(10 to 16 months)

Upper first molars
(13 to 19 months)

Lower first molars
(14 to 18 months)

Upper cuspids
(16 to 22 months)

Lower cuspids
(17 to 23 months)

Upper second molars
(25 to 33 months)

Lower second molars
(23 to 31 months)

The lungs, center of the respiratory system, expand in capacity, and the efficiency of air exchange improves as the child grows. This explains why an older child can exert herself without tiring as quickly as she did when she was younger. The upper respiratory tract — the throat and nasal passages — grows, too, during these years, but quite gradually. Because a very young child's respiratory passages are relatively short, germs have an easier time spreading than in the respiratory tract of an older child. And because the passages are relatively narrow, an infection that causes swelling creates blockages quickly. As the child grows and the passages lengthen and widen, the youngster becomes somewhat less vulnerable to respiratory-tract problems.

The immune system   Your youngster's immune system is actually a coalition of various parts of the body working together to ward off disease. Blood, skin and special tissue, called lymph tissue, are involved. Immunity improves with age as the different parts of the body function more efficiently. Your child will also develop antibodies — special substances to fight germs that do enter the body — making him less likely to succumb to every infection that comes along. However, the antibodies that your baby absorbed while in the womb and from breast milk will disappear, and he will need to be immunized against a number of diseases.

The reason youngsters tend to suffer an increase in colds and other minor infections when they enter nursery school or day care is that they are suddenly exposed to a host of new germs, or antigens, which their bodies are unprepared for. A healthy immune system will respond by stepping up the production of antibodies, so that your child's resistance will eventually overcome the new invaders.

Teeth   There is something undeniably charming about your 18-month-old's grin, which reveals about eight or 10 small, sparkling teeth. In the next year and a half, his smile will become positively dazzling as the remainder of the first set emerges *(box, page 29)*. These 20 primary, or so-called baby, teeth will carry your youngster through early childhood. When he is about six years of age, they will begin to loosen and fall out, to be replaced by 32 permanent teeth by around the age of 12.

Although your youngster will retain his primary teeth for a relatively few years only, they perform an important function. Aside from enabling him to speak properly and to chew all manner of foods, they establish the proper spaces for the permanent teeth and help them emerge correctly aligned.

Bones Your child's skeletal system is quite different from your own; his bones not only are smaller and softer, but more numerous as well. The newborn has about 350 "bones," some of which are not really bones at all but preformed models of bones made of cartilage, a soft but tough tissue. As the child grows, calcium is deposited in the cartilage models, and blood vessels bring in new bone cells. As these cells multiply, the cartilage hardens into true bone. At the same time, many of the developing bones knit together to form the 206 to 210 bones of the adult skeleton. The process, called ossification, is a lengthy one, and it is not completed until adulthood.

The bones of the body ossify in a specific order, at different times and rates. The skull bones knit together quite rapidly, and the soft spots, or fontanels, of a newborn's head disappear by the time the child is about 18 months old. On the other hand, the long bones of the youngster's legs will not fuse completely until the child is nearly 18 years of age.

After a child's skull has ossified, the bones of the arms and legs grow more rapidly than those of the trunk and head. It is this biological fact that alters your youngster's shape so dramatically in these years. The head, which in the newborn was a quarter of the child's length, represents only about one sixth of the first-grader's height. The six-year-old's legs, on the other hand, account for a greater portion of his body length than they did at birth.

Ossification in growth plates at each end of the bones produces the most easily apparent bone growth; it is responsible for your toddler's increases in height. During childhood, the bones also become thicker and shape themselves into the graceful forms that make up the mature skeleton. Meanwhile, a child benefits

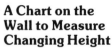

A Chart on the Wall to Measure Changing Height

"How tall am I growing?" and "How fast?" are important questions to every youngster. A personal height chart, marked on a wall at home, will give visible proof of a child's rapid growth and help her build a strong self-image. You can start measuring your toddler's height as soon as she is able to stand. Position her barefoot, back straight, with heels, buttocks and head touching the wall behind her. Place a book on top of her head as shown at left, to make sure that the measuring edge is parallel to the floor and at a right angle to the wall. Then mark and measure the child's height. Do this every six months or so for a permanent record of her growth. You may also find it fun to take a snapshot of her each time, so she can actually see how she has sprouted.

Alterations in a Young Child's Gait

Seeing your toddler walk is bound to be a matter of great pride to you as a parent. But it can also be a source of some concern if his gait remains awkward, or if his legs and feet assume odd shapes and positions after he seems to have mastered the business of walking. You may fret that his feet appear to be flat or lacking much of an arch, or that he walks pigeon-toed or duck-footed, or that he is bowlegged or knock-kneed.

The first thing to understand about these conditions is that they are for the most part perfectly normal and are likely to correct themselves in time. If your youngster's gait seems truly asymmetrical, however, or if your youngster complains of pain, of course, consult your pediatrician. But mainly you can relax and let nature do its work.

All babies seem to be born with flat feet, due to a pad of protective fat lying just beneath the arch. When your toddler starts to walk, the appearance of flatness will be accentuated by the fact that the ligaments of a child's feet at this stage are still not strong enough to support his weight. But within a few years the fat will disappear and the ligaments will tighten up to reveal the previously hidden arch. When your little one first walks he may also throw his feet out in a wide, duck-footed gait as he struggles to maintain a precarious balance. After a while, the reverse foot position may be true as he rolls along, toeing-in like a pigeon on stubby bowlegs. Bowleggedness generally starts to disappear around the age of two or two and a half.

But at the next stage, as his legs grow longer, the child may appear knock-kneed. The condition tends to occur between the ages of three and four, sometimes in combination with toeing-in, and may remain to some degree throughout the preschool years. Girls, because of their pelvic structure, seem more prone to knock-knees and seem to have them to a slightly greater extent. But knock-knees, too, are usually associated with normal bone growth and are usually self-correcting.

Other than being alert for genuine abnormalities, there is actually little for you to do except to make sure that your youngster has soft, well-fitting shoes in addition to plenty of chances to exercise his developing muscles and bones.

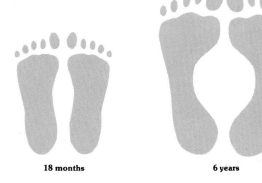

18 months   **6 years**

The six-year-old's footprints at right, above, show a strong arch, while those of the 18-month-old exhibit only the barest suggestion of an arch. But although the arch will often not be evident until the child reaches the age of six or so, it is there and would show up on an X-ray if one were taken. Parents can reassure themselves by observing the bottom of their youngster's feet as he stands on his toes; normally, the definite, longitudinal shape of the arch will appear on the sole.

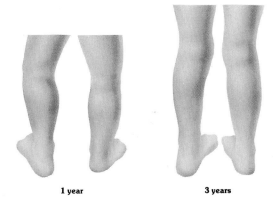

1 year   **3 years**

The legs at left, above, show the normal bowlegged stance of a year-old toddler. The condition, which seems to be a consequence of the child's restricted position in the womb, will gradually work itself out. Knock-knees (above, right) are common in older preschoolers. In some perfectly normal children the distance between the ankles can be as great as four inches when the knees are touching.

from the relative plasticity of his not fully ossified bones, because when damaged they mend much more quickly than bones that are completely hardened.

Muscles There are roughly 600 muscles in the adult body, accounting for about 40 percent of its total weight. An infant has the same number of muscles, but they are smaller and weaker, totaling only about 20 percent of her weight. As your child begins to use her body more actively, muscle fiber will thicken and become stronger, and it will attach more tightly to the bones, making movement more efficient.

Muscle growth helps explain why your youngster is likely to become thinner as she gets older. When a child reaches about four years of age, her muscles begin to grow faster than any other part of the body. This muscle growth accounts for more than half of the youngster's gain in weight. And firming abdominal muscles help flatten the round tummy that is the toddler's trademark. At the same time, fatty tissue accumulates more slowly than in earlier years of life, contributing to the slenderizing effect of muscle growth.

Balance and posture When your toddler first walks, he engages in something of a balancing act as he struggles to manage his ungainly body with its large torso and short legs. At this stage, to keep himself from falling, the child most likely adopts a clumsy-looking wide stance and a slightly swayed back. But be patient. As he grows taller and slimmer, his body proportions and center of gravity will shift, and he will be much steadier on his feet. Before long, if all goes well, the youngster's posture will be nicely erect and his stride sure and well-coordinated. The child's longer neck, squarer shoulders and flatter tummy all will add to the grace of his new posture *(page 34-37)*.

Another factor in the preschooler's improved posture is his more mature nervous system. A portion of the brain called the cerebellum is largely responsible for regulating posture and balance. The cerebellum receives messages about body position from peripheral nerves and makes minor adjustments to maintain the body's equilibrium. As your youngster grows older, the nerves of the extremities myelinate and thus are better able to transmit these messages to the cerebellum. With practice, this feedback system operates more and more smoothly. As a result, the child's posture and balance improve, and he no longer needs to devote total concentration to a simple act such as walking across the room. ❖

Getting an Early Start on Good Posture

Factors That Contribute to a Graceful Carriage

"Sit up straight" and "Stand up tall" are admonishments frequently given to children who slouch, as though simply by straightening up they could lick the problem. In fact, a youngster's posture is a product of many forces, including muscle tone and strength, balance, healthy skeletal development, nervous-system maturation and overall health habits.

The proper alignment of the body while sitting, standing and walking depends on how well the muscles work against the force of gravity to hold the body in balance. For these continuously working muscles to perform at peak efficiency, the individual needs sufficient nutrition, exercise and rest; indeed, a child will often respond to fatigue by slumping. Therefore, you should first of all make sure that your child gets plenty of sleep, healthful food and vigorous physical activity.

Good posture is best established during your child's formative years, when his body is still growing and developing, and he is acquiring habits for a lifetime. Not only does a graceful, upright carriage go hand-in-hand with self-esteem, it also leads to the equipoise that many physical educators, from basketball coaches to dance instructors, recognize as being a

Good Posture

In good posture, the head is held vertical, with the tips of the ears directly above the shoulders. The shoulders are back and relaxed; the chest is up and the lower abdomen is flat. The upper and lower back are slightly curved. Body weight is evenly supported by the feet, with the knees relaxed and the toes pointed forward.

Fair Posture

In a common deviation from the ideal posture, the head hangs a little bit forward and the chest is lowered slightly. The lower abdomen is still held in but is not quite flat, and the curves in the back have increased somewhat. More of the body weight is borne by the heels.

Poor Posture

When posture is poor, the head sags forward. The shoulder blades appear rounded or may project like stubs of wings. The belly protrudes and the curves in the upper and lower back are exaggerated. The pelvis tilts downward and the knees are pushed back in a bandy-legged stance. The distribution of body weight is too far back on the heels.

basic component of efficient movement.

But however important good posture may be to mind and body, parents should keep the subject in proper perspective. Posture evolves as a child grows, partly in response to subtle changes that occur in the curve of the spine throughout the early years. The body's center of gravity also shifts, as the trunk, head and limbs assume different proportions, producing further adjustments in the way a youngster holds himself. Today's doctors, realizing that postural irregularities often correct themselves as children grow, are less rigid than those of previous generations in their demands for upright carriage.

The illustrations on these pages provide examples of good and poor posture in standing and seated positions. To maintain good posture while walking, the body must retain the properties of good standing posture, with feet pointing forward and nearly parallel; the legs should swing freely, with heels touching first, and the arms should swing in opposition to the legs.

If, after studying these sketches, you feel that your child's posture does need improvement, some beneficial exercises that you can do together are demonstrated on the following two pages. ∴

Good and Bad Posture in a Chair

The slumped or semireclining style of sitting (far left) is quite common among children, but it encourages poor posture because it gives insufficient support to the spine and lower back. In the correct sitting position (left), the hips and back are flush against the chair, and the head and trunk are held erect. The knee joints should be bent at a right angle, and the feet should be flat on the floor with the toes pointed forward.

Good and Bad Posture on the Floor

The feet-and-hands-back pose (far left) is a position that many children like to take on the floor, especially when they are watching television. But sitting this way too frequently can exaggerate the normal mobility of the hip joints and ultimately may lead to the gait problem of toeing-in, or walking pigeon-toed. A youngster is better off sitting tailor style (left), with the trunk held erect and the legs crossed in front of the body.

Exercises for Improving Posture

The six exercises illustrated here are designed to stretch and strengthen the muscles in the neck, shoulders, stomach, back and legs. This type of conditioning can help improve a child's posture by developing the muscles that hold the bones and joints in proper balance.

Bear in mind that most normal, active children get comparable exercise in the course of everyday play. While the themes of exercise and physical fitness are excellent ones to introduce early, there is no need to embark on a concerted program of workouts unless you are particularly concerned about your child's posture. Even then, pursue the exercises only as long as the youngster is having fun.

You can further motivate your child by doing the exercises with him. Go slowly at first and introduce new routines only when he is ready. Make sure that your workout space is free of clutter so that you can safely move about. And when your child gets tired, end the session. ∴

Raising the Bridge   3 to 6 years

With the child on his hands and knees, have him lower his head to look back toward his legs. Tell him to raise his midsection slowly, pulling in his tummy and lifting his back. Count to five as he rises into an arch, have him hold it for five more beats, then let him relax for a count of five. Repeat the exercise seven times to strengthen the lower back and tummy.

Up on Toes   2 to 6 years

Help your child adjust his posture so that he is standing very straight with arms extended to his sides. Have him rise slowly onto his tiptoes, then descend just as slowly, for 10 repetitions. His chest should be up but not thrust out, and his back kept as rigid as possible. Once he has mastered this basic motion, have him practice walking across the room on his toes.

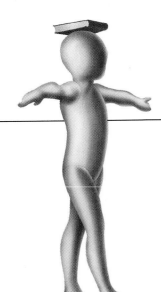

Posture Walk
3 to 6 years

*Have the youngster walk
with a paperback book balanced
on his head. Encourage him
to concentrate on keeping his
stomach and back as flat as
possible and his toes pointed
straight ahead as he walks.
Once he can keep the book balanced while walking forward,
have him try to do the same
while moving backward and
sideways or stepping over small
objects on the floor.*

Neck Stretching   3 to 6 years

*Have the child lie down flat on his back, with his arms at his sides
and his toes slightly pointed. Then have him lift his head up
and forward as far as he can: He should be able to glimpse his toes.
Have him hold that position for a count of 10 before lowering
his head. With practice, he can build up to a count of 20. This exercise helps develop the upper back, shoulders and neck.*

Balance Stand   4 to 6 years

*With the child standing, have him fold his arms across his chest,
then cross his legs. Ask him to bend his knees and descend
slowly, keeping his balance, until his bottom nearly touches the
floor. Then have him slowly rise again, all the while keeping his
arms and legs crossed and his feet in place. Encourage him to practice this difficult maneuver until he can repeat it three times.*

The Airplane   3 to 6 years

*Begin this back-strengthening exercise by asking the child to lie
tummy-down on the floor, with arms stretched out to the sides
and palms pointed downward. Have him raise his shoulders from
the floor while keeping his head and arms stiff and his feet
on the floor. Count to two and then have the youngster relax.
Repeat the sequence nine more times.*

2 Developing Movement Skills

Every parent who has ever watched a two-year-old in action knows that to a child movement is the very essence of life. In the space of a few minutes your youngster may play with one toy, drop it and pick up another, only to abandon both and dash across the room for a few fast gallops on his rocking horse. A moment later he is off again, flipping through a book, perhaps, or up-ending a tower of blocks. Turn your back for an instant and he may be gone from the room altogether, up the stairs and out of sight just as fast as his legs can carry him.

Movement is, of course, one way your child discovers himself and the world around him; and from the lumps and bruises he receives, he discovers his own physical limits as well. But no child is born with his movement — or large- and small-motor — skills fully developed. These emerge gradually during the early years of childhood, as your youngster's maturing nervous and muscular systems permit greater control over his body. In the process, the seemingly spasmodic movements of an infant become the stiff and uncertain toddle of the toddler, and eventually the poised and fluid running, jumping and climbing of the active six-year-old. In fact, by the time your child is six, he has achieved mastery of the basic motor skills; it only remains for him to refine them through practice and instruction to develop a wide range of new abilities — to roller skate and ski, for example, or to write in cursive script and play the piano. As with so many other aspects of parenting, your guidance and encouragement are the key ingredients in helping your child learn how to move with ever-increasing grace and assurance.

The Miracle of Motor Development

For the newborn the world is a tiny place, kept small in the early months by a baby's typically shallow field of vision and her limited ability to move around independently. As her eyesight improves and she learns to crawl and then to walk, your little one's horizons will expand appreciably. By the time she enters school her universe will have broadened to encompass the entire neighborhood and much of the community beyond; perhaps the youngster will even be navigating the route to and from her school on her own.

This remarkable metamorphosis — the evolution of a relatively helpless infant into a fully mobile, self-sufficient child of six — results partly from sheer physical growth and partly from the youngster's gradually expanding mental abilities. But perhaps the most dramatic and clearly visible landmarks along the way are the child's developing motor skills — her ever-growing ability to coordinate and control the large and small muscles of the neck and trunk, the legs and arms, the feet and hands.

The brain's control centers

All movement, however simple it may appear, is the result of a complex pattern of interaction among the various parts and systems of a child's body. Just to walk across a room, for example, your toddler must decide where and how fast to walk. He must also control his muscles, both to produce the appropriate movements and to maintain his balance, which shifts with every step he takes. At the same time he must use his eyesight to avoid obstacles and his sense of motion to provide feedback on his body's position, speed and direction.

Making all of this happen is the brain, which, like a puppeteer, initiates your youngster's every movement while simultaneously monitoring the information he is picking up about himself and his environment. Together, the brain and the spinal cord form the central nervous system, which includes five different control centers that dictate the child's every movement. The most highly developed of the control centers is the cerebral cortex, which is the outer layer of nerve cells enclosing the largest portion of the brain, the cerebrum. In the cerebral cortex sensory information is received and processed, decisions are made to move in a particular manner or direction, and the responses of various muscles to the brain's commands are analyzed and, as required, fine-tuned.

Buried inside the cerebrum lies another control center called the basal ganglia. Comprised of masses of neurons, it enables the child to initiate movements — such as swinging the arms when walking — without having to think first about them. Behind the basal ganglia, at the base of the cerebrum, is the third control center, the cerebellum, or little brain. The cerebellum governs locomotion and coordinates body movement. The fourth control center, the brainstem, connects the brain to the spinal cord. Among other things, it is responsible for winnowing information about the environment and relaying to the brain only as much as may be needed for action. The spinal cord constitutes the fifth control center, acting as a high-speed transmission line for nerve messages coming to and from the brain and the muscles.

Maintaining equilibrium   Complementing the central nervous system is the peripheral nervous system. It consists of sensory receptors located within the muscles, tendons, joints and the inner ear. These receptors constantly evaluate the body's position, direction and speed in order to maintain equilibrium. Together the central nervous system and peripheral nervous system coordinate movement by relaying appropriate impulses to the muscles and causing them to contract and relax to produce a desired motor response.

Before your youngster can become the master of his body's movements, he must have motor control. The development of motor control follows two separate but interrelated paths. The first involves the formation of gross-motor, or large-motor, skills — those that employ the large muscles of the body to produce such movements as walking and jumping. The second involves development of fine-motor, or small-motor, skills — small-muscle movements that require dexterity and precision. Included among the fine-motor skills are the motions needed to draw and write. But not every activity is so easily classified, and many of childhood's little pleasures, such as playing tag, are actually combinations of both gross- and fine-motor skills.

In terms of a youngster's overall physical development, gross-motor control precedes fine-motor control by months and even years, as evidenced by the fact that your child will use his leg muscles to walk long before he gains enough control of his hands and fingers to be able draw or manipulate a pair of scissors.

To watch a child's skills unfold is to behold one of nature's great action adventures. As the young neuromuscular system matures, one developmen-

A three-year-old displays a ball-catching pattern that reveals the still-developing nature of her motor skills. As depicted here, the child prepares to receive the ball by extending her arms stiffly, but flinches and loses track as it approaches. When the ball happens to land in her arms, she catches it by trapping it against her body.

tal trend after another asserts itself, enhancing and extending those that came before. But although virtually all children develop their motor abilities in the same predictable sequence, the age at which they acquire various skills will vary considerably; this is because the growth and development clocks of some children simply run faster or slower than others. Parents should be aware of these natural variations and not be concerned if their youngster seems not to be developing according to the timetable of another child the same age.

Refining skills   As your child's motor skills blossom, gradually allowing her greater control of her own body, they become the foundation for such basic movement skills as walking, climbing and kicking. These in turn provide the framework for the even more complex movements needed to participate in dance and sports activities.

But while many movement skills evolve naturally during early childhood as a by-product of growth and development, others must first be learned, then practiced. Consider, as an example, throwing a ball: The toddler's overhand throwing technique is underdeveloped at best, even in the most physically adroit two-year-old. Invariably, a child of this age displays little or no body rotation while throwing and keeps his feet fixed firmly on the ground; the ball itself is merely hurled forward in a simple back-to-front motion. But given proper instruction and enough practice, by the age of three and a half to five years the right-handed child is rotating his body slightly to the right in preparing to throw and then to the left in delivering the pitch, although his feet remain stationary.

Further practice leads to further refinement, and by six years of age the youngster is sliding one foot forward on the same side of the body as the throwing arm. But not until the child is six and a half or older does the mature, graceful ball-throwing pattern emerge as the youngster shifts his weight to the side holding the

The more coordinated five-year-old keeps her eyes on the ball as it approaches and skillfully prepares for the catch by extending her arms with her elbows bent but held loosely at her sides. The catch itself is accomplished with both hands.

ball, rotates his body in the windup, then transfers his weight to the opposite foot in delivery and finally whips the ball forward using both his arm and wrist.

Locomotor skills

There are three kinds of basic movement skills: locomotor, non-locomotor and manipulative. Of these, only the first, the loco-motor skill, involves the movement of the entire body from one place to another. Walking is a major motor development of infancy, the culmination of a series of postural changes that gradually bring your baby to her feet and set the stage for self-propulsion. Indeed, walking is the foundation upon which all other movement skills are based. Walking also permits your youngster to range farther in her explorations and to acquire new movement skills, as well. And since your child no longer needs her hands to help her get from one place to another, as she did during her earlier crawling days, her hands are now free to handle objects, thus allowing for the development of more complex manipulative skills.

Nonlocomotor skills

In contrast to locomotor skills, nonlocomotor skills involve more restricted movement — such as pushing and pulling, swinging and swaying, twisting and turning, falling and rising, bending and stretching. Essential to any of these activities, of course, is balance, and the gradual honing of nonlocomotor skills helps to exercise and refine the youngster's sense of balance. So important is the state of balance that it begins to develop during infancy; its progress can be traced in your baby's early ability to stabilize himself when he sits up and when he later rises to his feet for the first time. The sense of balance matures between the ages of three and five, and it continues to improve as the youngster grows older.

In balancing, children use their muscles to counteract such external forces as gravity and friction as they stand or move. This difficult task is accomplished with the aid of a constant stream of sensory data supplied by the eyes and the motion receptors of the peripheral nervous system. Working together, these detect even the most minuscule shift in balance, at the same time prompting the brain to initiate whatever movements are necessary to reestablish steadiness.

Manipulative skills

While the development of locomotor and nonlocomotor skills is critical to the individual's mobility, a child reaches his full movement potential in the skilled use of his hands and feet. Sophisticated manipulative skills, the third category of basic movement abilities, are among the unique gifts that distinguish humans from the lower animals. These skills make possible the handling and control of all kinds of objects, from blocks and balls to beanbags, scissors and pencils, as well as such fundamental childhood playtime activities as throwing, catching, kicking, bouncing, striking and rolling. Lacking fine-motor abilities, your child could not advance; she would be incapable of writing, drawing and even buttoning her clothes.

Since these and similar activities require a considerable degree of eye-limb coordination, they need time to mature. Thus while your one-year-old may attempt to kick a ball, he is not likely to kick it well until he is about five years old. In addition to promoting eye-hand and eye-foot coordination, manipulative skills are intricately related to the maturation of a youngster's cognitive abilities — his understanding of such concepts as size, shape, color and texture, as well as his awareness of space and his sense of timing.

Influences on motor development

A number of variables can affect motor development, including genetic factors, nutritional deficiencies, child-rearing practices, and cultural and ethnic differences. Low birth weight or malnutrition in infancy, for example, can impede motor development. But a supportive environment — one where barriers, physical or disciplinary, are few and all kinds of activities are encouraged — may enhance development by allowing the child greater freedom to explore and move about.

Gender differences in motor development also become apparent during the preschool years, with girls displaying more proficiency in skills requiring balance and body control — such as hopping, skipping and jumping — and boys performing better at throwing, catching and kicking, tasks that demand speed and strength. Behavioral differences between boys and girls are at least partly responsible for such gender discrepancies, since boys are more likely to participate in vigorous gross-motor exercises and girls to opt for less strenuous fine-motor activities. Cultural expectations also play a role in determining gender discrepancies, especially when parents encourage their sons to participate in traditionally masculine sports but exclude their daughters from such games.

Normal setbacks During the preschool years it is not unusual for a youngster to exhibit the mature pattern of a particular skill one day, only to regress the next day or to abruptly display an inexplicable lack of coordination. While fluctuating ability levels are normal at all ages, episodes of motor ineptness are particularly characteristic between the ages of three and four; these fluctuations may be traced to temporary lapses in control, often due to a lack of muscle coordination. Unfortunately, such lapses may give rise to emotional insecurity that can take the form of whining or become apparent when your usually independent three-year-old suddenly refuses to walk down the stairs without your help. To the parent who has grown used to a certain level of poise and dexterity in a child, such behavior may be alarming. But be assured that these temporary setbacks are fleeting, and in all likelihood the child who experiences them will soon be displaying even better motor control than she did before. ❖

Perspectives on Right- and Left-Handedness

Right-handedness and left-handedness have puzzled scientists for generations. Some researchers have ascribed right-brain dominance and heightened creative powers to left-handers, while other researchers have speculated that left-handedness is the result of birth trauma or early injury to the brain.

Today, most experts believe that hand preference has little relation to left- or right-cerebral dominance, and that it may instead be the result of heredity, cultural influences or even social pressures. Statistics show that 98 percent of children whose parents are both right-handed are themselves right-handed, while nearly half the children of two left-handed parents are left-handed. However, only 17 percent of boys and girls with one left-handed parent turn out to be left-handed.

The fact that most left-handed parents produce right-handed offspring seems to suggest that left-handedness may be a recessive trait. But this fails to prove that handedness is entirely hereditary: In many sets of identical twins, one of the youngsters is left-handed and the other youngster is right-handed.

In any case, a preference for one or the other hand often emerges very early in life, sometimes by the time an infant is three or four months old. This preference may come and go for years afterward, although by the time they are six years of age most children have become definitely right- or left-handed.

Less widely known is the fact that children can also exhibit a preference for one leg or one eye. When present, leg preference usually correlates with hand usage, but the condition is not so obvious or as widespread as hand preference. Using one eye more often than the other eye, however, is quite common.

Although much remains to be learned about the causes and effects of right- and left-handedness, the experts are nearly unanimous in advising parents not to force a child to use her right hand instead of her left or vice versa. Some of the experts believe that such interference in hand preference will not only frustrate the youngster but may even lead to emotional problems or to eventual reading difficulties. For that reason it is best to allow your child to follow her natural preference when it comes to handedness.

Endless Energy

Most children are whirlwinds of activity during the early childhood years. Younger children especially seem to be human dynamos, and it has often been observed of 18-month-olds, with their short attention spans and hair-trigger reflexes, that they think with their feet, dashing from here to there with reckless abandon, pausing at will to explore whatever catches their eye at the moment.

It is not surprising then that many parents consider their children to be overly active. According to one study, nearly half the mothers of a group of normal five-year-old boys thought their sons were excessively active, and more than one third of the mothers of a similar group of five-year-old girls felt the same way about their daughters. Indeed, the parents were convinced that their children's overactivity constituted a problem. But normal overactivity is not hyperactivity *(page 47),* and far from being a problem, the seemingly extraordinary energy resources of a young child are in fact quite ordinary.

Endowed with boundless energy, a toddler at play is a true study in motion, as these pictures of one 18-month-old demonstrate. In the space of minutes she gleefully took part in all the activities shown.

Once your youngster is able to walk, the world — or at least her own little corner of it — will quite literally be at her feet, as she scampers freely from one activity to the next. Within months she will add climbing, running, pushing and pulling to her repertoire of motor activities. Soon afterward the furniture and stairways that once loomed as obstacles will be as much a challenge as a jungle gym or slide in a park or playground. To your youngster it may suddenly seem that couches were made to be climbed, chairs to be pushed and toys to be dragged, and that every hallway is an indoor speedway — so much so that abrupt silence may become as alarming to you as a siren.

Trying to keep tabs on a motor-driven two-year-old is an exercise in futility for most parents, although it is comforting to know that time will take some of the steam out of your little one's engine. As she becomes older and her powers of concentration improve, your child's behavior will be less random and more purposeful. By the time she is three she will be capable of spending several minutes engrossed in a single activity before abandoning it for another. By the age of four she will exhibit even greater self-control. More coordinated than ever and also more self-confident, she will be eager and able to tackle

most motor tasks with abandon. At the same time, her increased attention span and rapidly developing manual dexterity will set the stage for the unfolding of a host of new small-motor skills — cutting straight lines with scissors, drawing crude stick figures, lacing shoes, fastening and unfastening buttons. Such skills pave the way for the more refined motor control of the five-year-old, whose physical poise and economy of movement make her appear to be less active than she really is.

And just what does all this movement mean to your child? At times it is merely a way to burn off excess energy — locomotion for the sake of locomotion. At other times movement is a joyous expression of a youngster's freedom from physical restraints, and on occasion, it may be a means of escaping some threat to personal safety.

More often, movement is a primary factor in self-discovery, especially during the first two years of life. Through her locomotor skills a child learns a variety of self-propulsion methods that in turn enhance her sense of independence. Those same skills also give her the mobility to explore the world around her and to bring her into contact with other people, thus encouraging the formation of healthy social behavior. Moreover, movement promotes balance, fosters the child's understanding of time and space and direction, and helps her to recognize her own limitations — for instance, that the arms and legs that carried her so easily to the top of the jungle gym may not so easily get her down.

Finally, movement is an important factor in the development of a child's self-image. Energetic activity provides a child the chance to exercise and improve her motor skills, and this helps her to approach group activities and new physical challenges confidently and competently — important factors in the development of healthy self-esteem. When a child is denied the opportunity for vigorous, free-wheeling exercise, the opposite can happen: Lacking confidence in her physical abilities, she may shy away from active play with her peers and thus, in a self-defeating cycle, further inhibit the development of her movement skills.

But if all children are normally overactive at some time or another, when are some children truly hyperactive?

The difficulty in answering that question is part of the reason many normal children have been mistakenly described as hyperactive by their parents or other observers. In gener-

al, true hyperactivity is characterized by frequent episodes of excessive and clearly inappropriate activity. It cannot be easily toned down, no matter how much parents or teachers might try. Hyperactivity is often accompanied by a number of behavioral and physiological symptoms, including temper tantrums, short attention span, aggressive or otherwise antisocial behavior, irregular eating and sleeping habits, easy distractibility and lack of coordination. School-age youngsters may also exhibit learning difficulties, especially language and reading problems.

In fact, hyperactivity sometimes goes unnoticed until a child is in school, although hyperactive children usually exhibit symptoms before the age of five. In some cases this is because the stress of attending school so aggravates the condition that it can no longer be ignored, even by those parents who might have suspected a problem earlier but chose to overlook it. In other cases it is simply because the disorder is finally recognized by a teacher who has had experience with hyperactive children.

Possible causes and treatment of hyperactivity

Hyperactivity has been attributed to a variety of factors, including birth trauma, food allergies, vitamin deficiencies, maturation delays, minimal brain dysfunction, lead poisoning and radiation exposure. Some studies have suggested that family discord and unrealistic parental expectations can intensify the problem, if not cause it. Research, however, has yet to verify any one of these factors, or a combination of them, as a cause.

The treatment of hyperactivity often involves medication for older children, but because of possible side effects — including insomnia, eating disorders and decreased cognitive abilities — drug therapy for preschoolers is controversial. In such cases, the best course of action is to entrust the youngster to a child psychiatrist or psychologist, who can assess the effect of a drug regimen or work with the child to help him modify his behavior.

Understandably, hyperactivity can have serious effects both on the child and on his relationships with family and peers. Patience and understanding will go a long way toward helping the child surmount the problem. Even so, the most tolerant of parents may at times feel overwhelmed by their youngster's hyperactivity. In such instances, more comprehensive measures than one-on-one counseling may be in order. A family-oriented psychotherapist or a support group, for example, might provide needed relief for child and parents alike. Managing learning difficulties requires the cooperation of the child's teachers, but parents will find that many schools today are prepared to meet the hyperactive child's special needs. ∴•

The Physically Fit Child

In an age when parents devote a part of each day to maintaining their own physical fitness, it is ironic that many neglect the fitness of their young children. As a result more preschoolers than ever are entering school in poor physical condition.

At the root of this neglect is the fact that over the years much of the attention to children's physical fitness was focused on the school-age child and on the adolescent. When the needs of the preschooler were addressed at all, it was too often erroneously. Some child-care experts in the early part of this century went so far as to caution parents that strenuous exercise could strain a young child's heart due to some imagined glitch in the development of the heart and vascular system. Today's misconception is that all children get ample exercise in the course of their everyday play.

A sturdy garden structure provides support for two youngsters engaged in an impromptu exercise session that will help build their strength and stamina. Because fitness is as important to the preschooler as it is to the older child, you should provide your little one with plenty of opportunities for vigorous outdoor play.

The importance of physical fitness

Adults exercise to improve cardiovascular fitness, reduce body fat, promote flexibility, enhance endurance and increase their muscular strength. It stands to reason, then, that children, even preschoolers, would realize many of these same benefits if given the chance. Since the preschool years are the years of phenomenal motor development, exercise can also play an important role in enhancing small- and large-motor control.

The components of physical fitness

Although the term "physical fitness" implies an overall state of conditioning, fitness is generally regarded as combining four elements. The first of these, muscular strength, refers to a child's ability to exert a single maximum effort during a particular exercise, as, for example, when lifting a heavy object. Muscular endurance, the second component of physical fitness, tests the youngster's capacity for repetitive exercise. The third component, circulatory-respiratory endurance, also involves repetitive exercise, except that here the activity is designed to place stress on the heart, lungs and vascular system. The final component, flexibility, measures the efficiency of various body joints. As might be expected, each of these four fitness components can be enhanced through exercises — activities that should be a part of the daily routine of every child but often are not.

Fitness activities

It is not always easy to assess a youngster's fitness without specialized equipment or undue inconvenience to the child. However, if your child is active much of the day in a variety of challenging physical activities, then it is probably safe to assume that she is fit. If, on the other hand, your youngster's daily life is essentially sedentary, with long hours spent inactive or in front of the television, then you should take steps to ensure that she receives the physical stimulation she needs.

Such activities need not be overly strenuous or unpleasant. For example, lifting and carrying large toys or other objects or swinging for several minutes on the monkey bars is sufficient to promote muscular strength. Muscular endurance will benefit from such familiar exercises as sit-ups, pull-ups and push-ups. Running, bicycle or tricycle riding and swimming are ideal ways to build up the circulatory and respiratory systems, while exercises that involve bending, twisting, turning and stretching will foster flexibility. In fact, many of the games and activities described on the following pages can very easily be combined to create a fitness regimen. Begun early, such a regimen will help establish a lifetime of good habits by enabling your youngster to develop a strong, healthy and highly mobile body. ∴

Fostering the Growth of Motor Skills

A child's first steps, first tricycle ride and first successful attempt at tying his own shoes are more than just memorable turning points in a family's life: These feats also mark important milestones in physical development. Although different youngsters may reach such milestones at different ages, a normal child's development proceeds in a generally predictable pattern. Most of the basic movement skills emerge by the age of five or six and are then refined throughout childhood and into adolescence.

Physical growth is largely responsible for the blossoming of these new skills. Bones lengthen to allow greater leverage, new muscle tissue gives the child added strength, and maturation within his nervous system quickens his reactions and improves his coordination. However, while physical growth is essential, exercise and practice are nearly as important if the youngster's physical abilities are to reach their full potential.

The following pages plot the usual course of motor development in children aged one to six and describe activities that will promote new skills and overall fitness. For each age group, there is a chart detailing the new milestones, followed by four pages of learning games and exercises. The first two pages of activities focus on large-motor, or gross-motor, skills — those governing the actions of the arms, legs, head and torso. The second two pages present games and exercises to improve the more manipulative, fine-motor skills. Instructions for making certain pieces of related equipment appear on pages 82-85.

Your youngster may reach particular milestones of physical ability much earlier or later than the ages indicated in the charts and yet still be well within the normal range. You should approach the activities with flexibility: Although they are based on the milestones for a particular age group, many of them can be enjoyed at other ages if you modify the rules to suit your child's developmental level. Be careful, however, not to push your youngster on to activities for which he is physically or mentally unprepared. To do so will only result in frustration.

The wide selection of activities included in this book is not meant to imply that small children need a thoroughgoing regimen of physical training; certainly, you should not expect your child to master every activity. The best approach is to introduce games and exercises on an occasional basis, choosing activities that are suited to your child's abilities and his level of physical maturity, so that he can practice new skills as they emerge. Look for activities that focus on his developmental strengths and weaknesses, then repeat the ones that he especially enjoys.

And however fun or beneficial you may consider an activity to be, never force your youngster to take part if he resists. He will profit from these games only if he participates with enthusiasm and enjoys the practice.

One to Two Years

Large-Muscle Control

- Crawls rapidly on hands and knees.

- Stands by 12 months and may take a few hesitant steps. Walks alone by 15 months and runs somewhat stiffly by two years.

- Can keep balance while walking one foot along the edge of a wide board.

- Avoids falls by quickly sitting down.

- Crawls up stairs; by 16 months, walks up the stairs, placing both feet on each step.

- When rising from a toddler-size chair, stands up without using hands.

- Climbs forward onto a chair and then turns around to sit.

- Kneels on the floor or on a chair.

- Pushes and pulls large objects such as strollers and boxes. Carries large toys.

- Stoops to pick up toys from the floor without losing balance.

- Responds rhythmically to music by moving whole body.

- Tosses a ball by 13 months; by 18 months, throws overhand without falling.

- Drops a ball into a basket.

- Kicks a ball by walking into it; cannot yet swing leg to kick.

Small-Muscle Control

- Picks up small objects with a pinching action of the thumb and forefinger.

- Retrieves small objects from a cup.

- Turns two or three pages of a book at a time.

- Beats two spoons together.

- Stacks a few blocks to make a tower.

- Scribbles randomly at 12 months, more de-liberately as the second year progresses.

- By 14 months, inserts a round block into a round hole; by 22 months, fits three different shapes into appropriate holes.

- Unzips zippers. Removes hat, shoes and socks independently.

- Feeds self finger foods, drinks from a cup, uses a spoon with growing skill.

- By two, holds two objects in one hand.

- Uses a stick or other object to retrieve a toy that is out of reach.

- Slips rings onto a pole.

- Turns knobs on appliances, such as stereos or televisions.

- Washes own hands and face and brushes hair with some success.

- Peels a banana. Unwraps packaged foods.

Large-Muscle Activities

Walking backward Once your child is walking on her own, you can help her further develop her new skill by teaching her how to walk backward — a challenge that will reward the youngster with increased balance.

Of course, you could merely walk backward yourself and encourage her to follow your example, but your toddler will have more fun if you approach it with some imagination. Taking her hands in yours, for example, you can pretend you are a tow truck and your child is a car, and walking backward, you can tow her to the garage. After a while, switch roles and let the child practice walking backward as the tow truck.

Pedaling As easy as this exercise is, it is also an excellent way to develop strength in your toddler's thigh, stomach and lower-back muscles. Start the exercise session by lying prone on the floor with your toddler stretched out on top of you, her back to your chest. Then with your legs in the air, pretend to pedal a bicycle and encourage your child to do likewise. At first, you may have to help the child by rotating her legs with your hands, but before long she will get the idea of the exercise and be pedaling on her own.

Rock and rhyme This rocking exercise *(below)*, which takes only a few minutes to do, is helpful in developing a child's arm and leg muscles. Standing face to face on a mat or carpeted area, take your toddler's hands in yours and sit down while she remains standing. Laying both of your feet gently on top of hers, rock the youngster back and forth while you recite "Hickory, Dickory, Dock" or some other favorite nursery rhyme or song.

Paper-bag blocks Grocery-bag blocks are fun to create and make surprisingly sturdy playthings for young children. They can be kicked, thrown and pushed without harming your walls, furniture or other children, or they may be used as oversize building blocks.

Making the blocks is an easy and absorbing rainy-day activity for parent and child. For each block, you will need two large grocery bags and 14 or so double-page sheets of newspaper. Show your child how to crumple the newspaper into balls, then open one grocery bag and fill it nearly to the top with the newspaper balls *(above)*. Slip the second bag over the first and tape it in place.

Tunnel roll The younger toddler, when first learning to play ball, can begin to develop her throwing and catching skills by rolling a large ball through a two-foot-wide "tunnel." To make the tunnel, stand in front of your child with your feet wide apart; have another player sit behind you. Give your child a large ball and encourage her to roll it through the space between your feet by pushing it with both hands. The other player should then roll the ball back to the youngster. Whether your child catches the ball or not, be sure to praise her efforts. As her aim improves with practice, you can make the game more challenging by standing with your feet closer together.

If a third player is not available, you can make the tunnel out of two columns of carefully stacked blocks or books with a yardstick placed across them. You will then be free to be the catcher.

Jack-in-the-box A child is asked to mimic a jack-in-the-box in this activity, encouraging the youngster's natural inclination to learn by imitating the actions of others. Moreover, in repeatedly go-

ing through the motions of a jack-in-the-box, your child can develop her sense of timing. Start by sitting on the floor across from your toddler with your knees bent out and the soles of your feet touching; clasp your ankles with your hands. Then, to the music of "Pop Goes the Weasel" or some other favorite song, bend all the way forward, sitting up suddenly at the refrain of the song. As a variation, you can pop up on the count of three. After demonstrating the activity several times, encourage your toddler to follow your example and join in the fun.

Pull toys Children of all ages like to pull toys around the house; the more noise the toy makes, the more the child seems to like it. Moreover, as she maneuvers the pull toy around corners and up the stairs, the child is improving her balance and coordination. Such pull toys need not be store-bought, since with a minimum of effort and a little imagination many common household items — including metal measuring cups, jar lids, yogurt cups, spools, hair rollers and cardboard tubes — can be strung together to make toys that your child can drag around to her heart's content. Round ice-cream or oatmeal cartons, filled with macaroni and then taped closed with extra-strong fiber tape, can also be strung together to make a toy that rattles as it moves. Or try decorating shoe boxes and then connecting them with string to form a train.

Dowel activities The following three exercises, all of which can help improve a child's muscular strength and coordination, require the use of a ¾-inch wooden dowel about two feet in length. An old broom handle will also do nicely.

The first is a simple rowing exercise in which you and your toddler use the dowel as a make-believe oar. Sit on the floor facing your child with her legs outstretched between yours. Have her grasp the dowel with both hands and hold it out in front of her. Place your hands on top of hers so that both of you are holding the dowel. Then lean alternately backward and forward as you pretend to row a boat, timing your strokes to the rhythm of "Row, Row, Row Your Boat" or other songs.

For the second exercise, sit across from your toddler with your legs crossed. Holding the dowel between you in the same manner as before, both of you should dip together — first to the left and then to the right — without lifting your bottoms off the floor. This sequence, which teaches a child to move in coordination with another person, should be repeated a dozen times or more.

Finally, by using a dowel to suspend your toddler in midair *(above),* you help strengthen her hand, arm and upper-body muscles. Begin by standing face to face. Let your toddler hold onto the dowel with both hands, arms outstretched, then cover her hands with your own. Slowly lift her into the air about four inches off the floor and let her hang for a count of eight before lowering her to the floor. Repeat several times. As your toddler gains confidence, encourage her to extend her legs out in front of her while hanging. This will strengthen abdominal muscles as well.

Rope step-over This activity is designed to increase a child's spatial awareness and improve her balance. Take a length of rope and drape it over two chairs so that the rope hangs about an inch off the floor. Do not tie the rope to the chairs, because the child could trip over it and tumble to the floor along with the chairs. Show your toddler how to step over the rope, then allow her to try. As she becomes more skilled, you can gradually raise the level of the rope to a maximum of six inches *(below).* ⁂

Small-Muscle Activities

Plunker The simple-to-make, noisy-to-play game of plunker is also an exercise in manual dexterity. File smooth and tape the edge of an empty coffee can where the metal top was removed. Then cut an X in the plastic lid and replace it on the can. Give the youngster a supply of large beads, milk-jug lids or similar objects too large to be swallowed. Show her how to push them one by one through the X in the coffee-can lid *(above)*. As the objects strike the bottom of the can, they resound with a child-pleasing "plunk" that will keep your toddler happily entertained. Moreover, in pushing the objects through the X, she must overcome the resistance of the plastic lid, thereby strengthening hand muscles.

Dip and find Young children take great pride in finding hidden objects, and this hiding game also offers the opportunity to practice manual skills. Moreover, this game helps teach a youngster that just because something disappears from sight does not mean it no longer exists, and that objects of one size can often be fitted inside larger objects.

　　To get started, fill a small box, pail or other container with crumpled balls of newspaper. You can show your child how to crumple newspapers, a good way to exercise her fingers and hands. Then, as your toddler watches, bury a small toy in the paper and allow her to

search for it. When she finds it, praise her success, then ask her if she wants to try again. Most likely she will.

First jigsaw puzzle The older toddler who has spent months playing with blocks and containers may already have a rudimentary understanding of shapes and sizes. You can build on that understanding and help your child develop her manipulative skills by fashioning a jigsaw puzzle out of sheets of ordinary construction paper.

　　In the beginning, make it easy for the child by cutting a square from one edge of the construction paper. Show her how the square fits into the space it was cut from, then let her try. Follow this by cutting out a triangle from the edge of another sheet of paper and repeating the sequence of trial-and-error fitting. Continue cutting out other shapes and letting the toddler try to match the cutout shapes to the spaces.

　　As your youngster's competence increases, you can make the puzzles more challenging by cutting shapes from the centers of the sheets rather than from the edges. Once you have several puzzles cut out, give her the paper frame for the square and a variety of cutout shapes to try fitting into it. Encourage her to find the square piece to fit the square shape. Do not intervene, however, if she tries to squeeze the triangle into the square, since children learn from their mistakes as well as from their successes.

Finger puppets Playing with finger puppets *(above)* is an activity that children can begin enjoying by the time they are one year old. Among its benefits are improved finger dexterity and communication skills, as well as the opportunity to develop youthful imaginations by pretending the puppets are real or imaginary characters and using them to act out stories.

You can make puppets like the ones shown by cutting fingers from gloves, a thumb from a baby's mitten for your little one and a finger from a gardening glove for you. Sew on felt faces and add hair made of yarn, and you will have the makings for hours of shared fun.

Shape matching This early matching activity *(above)*, designed to improve eye-hand coordination and spatial awareness, is best suited to older toddlers who are close to their second birthday. Begin by gathering up a number of household items that are too large to be swallowed, such as spoons, jar lids, canning rings and combs. Then, using a felt-tip marker, trace around each object onto a large sheet of cardboard. Place the objects in a pile, mix them up and let the child fit them one by one into the correct shapes outlined on the cardboard. Provide lots of encouragement and only as much help as she needs.

Zipper This simple activity will let your child exercise her wrist muscles. Put on a sweater or jacket with a zipper tab large enough for her to grasp firmly, kneel to your child's level and then let her pull the zipper up and down repeatedly. As she moves the zipper you can describe whether it is open or closed, up or

down, and she will learn new words in the process. Try the same game using large buttons on a sweater. It is easier for a young child to practice on a knitted garment because the buttonholes tend to expand a little.

Pegs in holes A few empty spools of thread and several drinking straws are all you need to set up this toddler-size version of a pegboard game *(below)*, an excellent means to increase concentration and eye-hand coordination. Before starting, cut the straws to half their length and make sure they slide easily into the spools. (Full-length straws standing in spools would be more likely to poke into the eyes of a toddler bending over a table.) Then stand the spools on end and show your youngster how to insert a straw into the hole of one spool. Encourage her to do the same with another spool. Once she gets the idea, let her continue fitting the rest of the straws into the remaining spools. In time, you can make the activity a bit more challenging by slipping a straw into one spool and then adding another spool to form a tower. Have your child make several others to match it with the remaining spools and straws. ⁘

Two to Three Years

Large-Muscle Control

- Jumps in place.

- Can walk backward five to 10 feet in a straight line.

- Runs well. Stops and starts easily.

- Kicks ball with a vigorous forward swing of the foot; backswing and follow-through are still somewhat awkward.

- Climbs confidently up and down furniture to look out a window.

- When lying down, can raise himself to a standing position without pulling himself up on chair, table legs or other support.

- Walks on tiptoe a few steps by the age of two and up to 10 feet by two and a half.

- Balances momentarily on one foot.

- By two and a half years of age, climbs stairs alternating feet from step to step. May still place both feet on the steps while descending.

- Jumps from the bottom step of a flight of stairs, landing upright.

- Seats self smoothly on a chair.

- Can climb into a box without assistance.

- Pedals a tricycle by two and a half years.

Small-Muscle Control

- Consistently favors one hand for most activities.

- Following an adult's example, draws curved, horizontal and vertical lines.

- Can open doors by their handles.

- Turns pages of a book one at a time.

- By two and a half years old, holds a pencil with thumb and forefinger instead of gripping it with a fist.

- Snips with scissors around the edges of a piece of paper, but does not yet cut along a straight line.

- Stacks three blocks in order to form a kind of pyramid.

- By the age of three, builds a tower 10 blocks high.

- Pulls, pounds and squeezes clay.

- Folds and creases paper.

- Unscrews caps from bottles and jars.

- Can turn the handle of an egg beater.

- Undresses self completely and begins to dress independently. Sometimes manages to button a button.

- Feeds self skillfully with a spoon and begins to have some success with a fork.

- Dries hands with a towel.

Large-Muscle Activities

Palm paddles Most children enjoy batting balls or balloons around with their hands, even though the combination of a toddler's small hands and his limited coordination virtually guarantees more misses than hits. A child's normal physical growth will eventually reverse that ratio, but in the meantime you can equip him with a set of palm paddles *(below)* to make it easier for him to hit the target.

Making the paddles requires heavyweight paper plates, some elastic, and a needle and thread *(page 83)*. Once the paddles are made, slip one on your youngster's hand and another on your own and use the paddles to bat a balloon back and forth. You can also show your child how to bat the balloon vertically into the air several times in succession to keep it from hitting the ground, counting each hit aloud in order to give him some practice in number skills. In any case, be sure to supervise balloon play; a burst balloon can frighten a young child, and a deflated balloon is a potential choking hazard.

Balance ropes In this safe version of walking a tightrope *(above),* the rope is laid directly on the floor, so that there is no chance of the youngster falling off and injuring himself. The rope may be stretched straight across the floor or placed in any number of configurations to make walking it more challenging. To enhance the tactile stimulation, let your child walk the rope barefoot. Later, as his competence increases, you can encourage him to walk backward or sideways on the rope as well as forward, or you can place small obstacles along the rope for him to step over. Developing a sure sense of balance is a prerequisite to a number of later games and activities in which your child will participate.

Magic yarn Using leftover strands of yarn, you and your toddler can create a variety of shapes and mimic them with body positions for increased body and spatial awareness. Cut the yarn into strands about two feet in length. Explain to your youngster that this is magic yarn that you will use to make shapes, and that you can copy these shapes with your own body.

Each of you should first take a length of yarn. Sit down on the floor and make a shape with your strand, then contort your body into the same shape. Have your child do the same, first with the yarn and then with his body. After a while you can vary the activity by challenging each other: One of you makes the magic shape with the yarn while the other copies it with his body.

Bridges and tunnels Show your child how to make bridges and tunnels with his body, a feat enabling him to expand his spatial awareness and explore the concepts of "over" and "under" as he exercises large muscles. Chances are your two-year-old already knows what bridges and tunnels are, although if he does not, you can show him pictures of them as you explain their purpose. Using your body, show your toddler how to make a bridge or tunnel, by standing with your legs apart to form a tunnel or by kneeling

and bending over, with your head and arms on the floor, to make a bridge. Allow him to crawl through the tunnel or climb over the bridge *(above),* then suggest that he use his own body to make a bridge or tunnel. When he does, you can make a toy truck or stuffed animal go over or under him.

Jumping games A child's ability to jump marks a major milestone in the development of his large-muscle skills. Practice in jumping will strengthen his leg muscles while improving his balance and coordination.

To prevent injury, limit the height from which your child jumps, having him stand on a thick, hardbound book or perhaps the bottom step of a flight of stairs. Show him how to get more spring into his jump by starting out with his arms held back and then swinging them forward as he jumps. You can make a game out of jumping by laying a rope on the floor and having the child jump back and forth over it; later you can vary the activity by showing him how to jump backward or sideways over the rope.

Wilderness hike You can give your youngster's muscles a workout as you take him on an excursion into a make-believe wilderness. Along the way he will be exploring the concepts of "over," "under," "in," "out" and "on" as well as developing his crawling, climbing and jumping skills. The only equipment necessary is some rope or heavy twine and an active imagination.

Begin by laying one end of a six-foot length of rope on a chair and letting the other end trail across the floor. Place a second six-foot rope loosely on the floor in another part of the room and lay two three-foot lengths of rope parallel to each other in yet another spot. Choose a particular wilderness area and describe the scene to your child as you set out on your adventure: the hot sun blazing over-

head, perhaps eagles nesting in the high tree branches, bears patrolling the underbrush and deer emerging to drink at the ponds.

You and your youngster can create any number of obstacles on your hike around the room. For example, the rope on the chair can be lifted from the floor to become a log to jump over or a fence to crawl under, while the two parallel three-foot lengths can be a stream to cross or a narrow pass between two cliffs. The remaining six-foot rope can be circled on the floor to form a make-believe lake or stretched out to form a pretend rope-bridge across a raging river. With each subsequent pass through the "wilderness," you can devise new ways to make use of the ropes.

Bubbling up This jumping game, suited for birthday parties or other group occasions, requires several children — the more the merrier. Parents, too, should feel free to join in. Each participant pretends he is a bubble in a pot of boiling water. First he hops around the play area, "bubbling up." When one bubble touches another one, they become united and must then jump around together, until all the bubbles are hopping around the room as one.

Pretzel Your child can strengthen his abdominal muscles while increasing his flexibility with this easily performed exercise. Sit across from him with legs outstretched in front of you to demonstrate. Taking your left foot in both hands, raise it to touch your nose *(below),* then repeat with the right foot. Encourage your child to alternate left and right feet with you a dozen or more times. ⋰

Small-Muscle Activities

Play-dough puzzles   Homemade jigsaw puzzles can be created out of clay or play dough *(above)*. Roll the play dough one-half inch thick on a table or countertop and use different cookie cutters to cut out a variety of shapes. Help the youngster to match the cutouts to the proper spaces in the dough; if necessary, show him how to turn the shapes around until they slip easily into the correct holes. Once the puzzle is complete, let your child remove the pieces and try all over again.

Rings and hooks   For this activity, you will need to make a hook-board from a piece of cardboard and plastic cup hooks with stick-on backs *(page 83)*. Then show your youngster how to hang canning-jar rings or rings cut from the plastic tops of margarine tubs on the hooks. As he does, he will be developing his manipulative skills and coordination. When the large rings become too easy for your child, you can increase the challenge of the activity by providing new plastic lids with smaller holes cut in them.

Magnet fishing   Let your toddler go fishing in a cardboard carton or plastic bucket. To make the tackle, use a stick or dowel no more than one foot long and a string no longer than three feet. Tie one end of the string to the stick and tie a small horseshoe or bar magnet to the string's other end. Metal jar-lids placed in the bottom of the box or bucket make splendid fish. Your youngster will improve his eye-hand coordination as he sinks the magnet into his makeshift lake and snags as many big ones as he can.

Finger plays   Finger plays — short verses acted out with the fingers — can help your youngster to improve his dexterity. Since the child is also committing the verses to memory, he will be practicing his retention skills at the same time.

There are countless finger plays to choose from, many of them handed down from generation to generation. Among the favorites are these two:

Ten Fingers
I have 10 little fingers. (Extend the 10 fingers.)
They all belong to me. (Point to self with forefinger.)
I can make them do things. (Wave the 10 fingers around.)
Would you like to see?
I can open them up wide. (Spread fingers apart.)
Shut them up tight. (Clench fists.)
Put them out of sight. (Place hands behind back.)
Jump them up high. (Raise hands, fingers extended.)
Jump them down low. (Lower hands, fingers pulled in.)
Fold them quietly. (Fold them in lap.)
And sit just so. (Sit down, hands folded.)

Dig a Little Hole
Dig a little hole. (Make a digging motion with your fingers.)
Plant a little seed. (Mimic dropping a seed in a hole.)
Pour a little water. (Pour.)
Pull a little weed. (Pull up and throw away.)
Chase a little bug. (Make a chasing motion with hands.)
Heigh-ho, there he goes! (Shade eyes.)
Give a little sunshine. (Cup hands, lift to the sun.)
Grow a little rose. (Pick a flower, smell it, smile.)

Clay play   Most children enjoy playing with clay; at the same time, all that pounding, squeezing and pulling provide excellent exercise for little hand muscles. Play dough is more malleable and easier for young children to work with, and it is available in many toy and variety stores. Or you can make your own version by mixing two cups flour, one cup salt and two tablespoons cream of tartar in a pot. Add one tablespoon oil and two cups water — and a few drops of food coloring if you like — and stir over medium heat until the mixture is thick and blended. When ready, remove the mixture

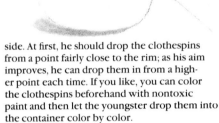

from the pot and cool it until it can be handled, then knead out any lumps in the dough. Store the play dough covered with plastic wrap in the refrigerator.

You should not expect your two-year-old to turn out elaborate works of art with his clay or play dough. At this age, it is enough that he enjoy the clay purely as a sensory experience. So start by showing him how to roll a lump of clay into a ball and pound it flat, or how to roll a ball of clay into a snake. You can also give the youngster a plastic knife, cup or cookie cutters and help him cut shapes from flattened clay.

Clothespin play   Wooden clothespins of the old-fashioned, push-on variety make inexpensive yet intriguing pieces of play equipment for young children. Used in conjunction with a bowl, cannister or plastic jar, the clothespins can be manipulated in several ways to foster the development of a youngster's eye-hand coordination and manual dexterity.

Get your child started by showing him how to drop the clothespins into the container one by one *(below)*. The opening should be large enough for the child to put his hand in-

side. At first, he should drop the clothespins from a point fairly close to the rim; as his aim improves, he can drop them in from a higher point each time. If you like, you can color the clothespins beforehand with nontoxic paint and then let the youngster drop them into the container color by color.

For a second activity, ask your youngster to fit the clothespins onto the rim of a bowl *(above)*. Do not be surprised if this turns out to be a relatively complex manual maneuver for someone his age. Again, painted clothespins offer the chance to make the activity a lesson in colors as well as dexterity.

Unscrewing lids   Children like to test their abilities to unscrew jar lids and screw them back on again. You can build on this interest by giving your youngster a large screw-top plastic jar — large enough for his hand to fit easily inside — and encouraging him to fill the jar with small toys and other objects. Let him unscrew the lid, fill the jar, screw on the lid, unscrew again and dump the objects out. Make sure that all objects are too large to be swallowed. Such play will help develop a youngster's manual dexterity and strengthen his muscles, while enlarging his understanding of the concepts of "in" and "out" and "off" and "on."

Squeeze and dribble   Filled with a salt-and-flour mixture, plastic squeeze bottles can be a source of fun as well as good exercise for little hands and wrists. To make the dribble mixture, blend equal parts of salt, flour and water. Add some liquid nontoxic paint to tint the mixture, blend well and pour into a squeeze bottle. Repeat the process using additional bottles and other colors, if you like. Then show your youngster how to squeeze the mixture out in dribble patterns on sheets of cardboard, mixing and matching colors to suit his fancy. The creations should be left to dry for a day on the cardboard if you wish to keep them. ∴

Three to Four Years

Large-Muscle Control

- Stands with heels together, arms at side, without losing balance.

- Turns corners and rounds obstacles at a running pace.

- Hops on one foot and begins to show preference for one foot over the other.

- Balances on one foot for up to five seconds.

- Can walk along a board or curb placing one foot in front of the other.

- Throws a ball overhand six to 10 feet. Uses shoulder and elbow when throwing.

- Catches a large ball by holding arms stiff in front of body.

- Can carry an object on a tray without dropping either.

- Jumps one foot or farther from a standing start.

- Pedals around wide corners on a tricycle.

Small-Muscle Control

- Draws crude circles.

- When given an incomplete drawing of a human head and body, will add at least two body parts without prompting.

- Uses scissors to cut a sheet of paper in half.

- Stirs a liquid with a spoon.

- Can pick up small objects with tongs.

- Builds a pyramid that includes six blocks.

- Threads large wooden beads on a string.

- Winds up toys.

- Pours from a pitcher into a cup.

- Becomes more efficient in the use of a fork, but needs to hold it with a fist.

- Unbuttons front buttons by the age of three. Unbuckles belts by three and a half.

- Washes and dries hands independently.

Large-Muscle Activities

Jumping through hoops By the time they are three, many children are expert jumpers, but even experts enjoy putting their skills to the test. To give your child a jumping game, lay one or more hoops on the floor or ground as a target, or outline circles in chalk on cement. Suggest to your youngster that she jump into a circle and then out of it again several times in a row, as she gradually moves around the circle. As soon as your child masters this skill, you can show her how to jump from one circle to another, or how to jump from a low height — such as a small stool or bottom stairstep — into a circle. Exercises such as these enhance a youngster's strength, coordination, balance and agility.

Steppingstones This enjoyable exercise in eye-foot coordination uses carpet samples at least 12 inches square, which most rug stores sell for a nominal fee. Get samples with a skidproof rubber backing. Spread them on a nonslippery surface, such as a carpeted floor, spacing them some 12 to 24 inches apart or as far as your child can comfortably step or leap. Then let her pretend they are steppingstones through a creek or mudbank *(below)*. The carpet-sample "stones" can be placed in various configurations, which can be changed to form a different path each time your youngster enters a new imaginary terrain. For a further variation, give her a ball to hold as she steps or jumps from stone to stone.

Tumbling fun Some youngsters show little interest in tumbling activities or are afraid of hurting themselves, but many three-year-olds need little encouragement to perform floor stunts. Timid children should never be forced to participate beyond their abilities and inclinations. In any case, for your child's safety, be sure that she confines her tumbles to a carpeted floor or a mat. At first, you may have to walk your youngster through the following activities, but she will soon catch on and perform the stunts on her own.

Have her try the logroll to improve her coordination and strengthen her trunk muscles. Ask her to lie flat on her back with her arms extended overhead and her hands clasped. Then tell her to roll to the right and left like a log. For the egg roll *(above)*, the child should lie on her back, bring her knees to her chest with her hands, then roll like an egg in every possible direction.

In order to accomplish a forward roll, your child should squat with her hands on the mat in front of her. Tell her to tuck her chin into her chest and bring her head down to the floor. Then, making her body round like a ball, she should roll forward into a sitting position. Be sure to spot your child — guide her with your hands — so she can move smoothly and securely. For the forward roll, kneel beside her and place one hand on the back of her neck and the other hand under the backs of her thighs. The pressure of your hand on her neck will help her to maintain her rounded shape. A little lift from your other hand will help her get her legs over.

Scooping balls In this catching game, you and your child scoop up a rolling ball using plastic scoops fashioned from bleach or milk containers *(page 84)*. Give one scoop to your child and take another one yourself. Sit on the floor facing each other about six feet apart. Then, holding

the scoops flat on the floor as targets, roll a small rubber ball back and forth toward each other's scoops. If your youngster's aim is off, move your scoop to catch the ball. As she aims and rolls the ball, your child will be exercising her eye-hand coordination skills.

Bop the clown Throwing objects at an amusing target *(above)* is a favorite of children of all ages. Draw a clown face on a large piece of cardboard. Prop the face against a wall or other support and give your child one or more beanbags or balls. Encourage her to hit the clown anywhere at all at first, and later to aim for one particular place, such as the nose, mouth, hat or cheeks. Instruct your child to fix her eyes on the place she wants to hit and not on the hand holding the beanbag or ball. Eye-hand coordination is the objective, along with improving your child's throwing skills.

Ball pass Several children are needed for this activity, in which a ball is passed around a group seated in a circle. Give the ball to one youngster and tell her to roll or push it to the child next to her; that child then sends the ball on to the next. After a while, you can introduce a second ball into the circle and later still, you can have them stand in a circle and toss a ball — the sponge type is best — from child to child. Again, you can add a second ball to the circle as the children grow more proficient at throwing and catching.

Spaceship Indoors or out, the game of spaceship is best performed with a number of children. Begin by choosing an object to represent the earth — a tree if outdoors or perhaps a soft chair indoors. The children are the spaceships, clustered at the start around the earth. Count down from five out loud, and when you call out "Blast off!" they should take off from earth and pick up speed, eventually racing in orbit around the earth while avoiding collisions with one another. After they complete a number of orbits, command the spaceships back to a splashdown on earth.

Floor crossings As your three-year-old has no doubt already discovered, there is more than one way to cross a room. This activity will give her a good workout as she explores different means of locomotion. First, remove all furniture and other obstacles from the center of the play area and have your child sit at one end of the room. Then, at your signal, have her cross the floor in the manner you specify. You may, for example, tell her to jump on both feet or slither on her belly like a snake. She might also leap or roll across, slide forward or backward in a sitting position, or walk on her knees or in a squatting position. In addition, you might ask her to take giant steps, walk on her heels or tiptoe. For still more variety, she can cross the floor like a robot or a monster or pretend that she is very small.

Ring toss This child's version of horseshoes offers your youngster an opportunity to practice throwing at a target only a short distance away *(below)*. If you do not own a ring-toss game, you can make one by pressing an eight-inch long dowel into a block of florist sponge. Do not place this block directly on carpeting: The dye in the sponge may run. Give your child a few rings to toss at the stake — or stakes, if you set up several. You can use canning-jar rings or rings cut from corrugated cardboard or from the plastic tops of margarine tubs. Encourage your child to keep her eyes on the stake as she tries to circle it with the rings, rather than looking down at her hands. If it is too difficult for her at first to circle the stake, make the objective to get as close to the stake as possible. ⋰

Small-Muscle Activities

Humpty Dumpty pretzels This activity exercises manipulative skills with the aid of a bag of twisted pretzels. Remove two or three pretzels from the bag and break them into several large pieces. Scramble the pieces and help your youngster put the pretzels back together *(below)*. As she displays more competence, you can create more complex pretzel puzzles simply by breaking up more pretzels. To reward your youngster's successes, let her munch on the completed pretzel puzzles.

Stringing beads A great deal of concentration is required for a child to string beads or other objects onto a shoelace *(above)*. Perseverance is rewarded, however, with improved manual dexterity and eye-hand coordination, as well as a decorative string of beads to display. Large wooden beads are easiest for your youngster's little fingers to handle. However, you can easily substitute a number of common household items for the beads, including empty spools of thread, dry macaroni, large washers and giant paper clips.

Pitcher pouring By the time your youngster reaches her fourth birthday, she may be displaying some skill in pouring liquid from a pitcher into a cup, although there will inevitably be some spills. You can help her develop her skill at pouring early by giving her the chance to practice where spills will not matter — in the sandbox. Using a play shovel, dig a hole in the sand, shoveling the sand into a plastic bucket or pitcher. When the container is almost full, show your child how to pour the sand from the bucket or pitcher back into the hole. Then let her have a try.

Once your youngster gets the hang of the activity, introduce a second plastic container and let her practice pouring the sand from one to the other.

Pickup sticks Unlike the game you may have played as a child, this game challenges a youngster to use two wooden ice-cream sticks to pick up small objects. Set out some blocks, small stuffed animals or corks, and see if your child can pick them up one at a time and deposit them in a box or basket a few yards away. Younger children may find this activity somewhat difficult, but as your preschooler nears her fourth birthday, she will find the game more and more enjoyable.

Toothpick pegboards Pushing pegs onto a pegboard gives a child the opportunity to develop the pincer grasp that she will later use to hold a pen or pencil. You can buy a pegboard set if you wish, but a substitute can be made using plastic toothpicks and a block of plastic foam or florist sponge. In either case, and especially if you are using toothpicks, you will need to supervise your child carefully in order to avoid accidental poking or choking. Once your youngster understands how to use the pegboard, show her how to create a pattern on the board by making a straight line across the top or down one side, or by using the pegs to outline a particular letter or shape. You can also run a line of pegs of different colors across the top of the board and encourage your youngster to match the colors in a second line of pegs. Placing pegs on the board with one or both hands and removing them quickly in the same manner will further enhance your little one's manual dexterity.

Spooning beans By the time she is three, your child will be fairly adept at handling a spoon, and spooning beans from one container to another will allow her to practice that skill *(below)*. Begin the activity by providing the child with a variety of dried beans — kidney beans, limas, lentils and black-eyed peas are readily available in most supermarkets.

Place each kind of bean in a small plastic bowl or cup and show your youngster how to spoon a layer of one kind into an empty jar. Encourage her to add a second layer of a different bean and then a third and a fourth, until the jar is full. You can suggest when it is time to change kinds of bean. But do not force the issue if her idea of layering is not the same as yours; compliment her on her creation, however it may turn out.

Be certain, too, to supervise your little one carefully during this activity; young children sometimes experiment with sticking beans in their nostrils or ears. As a variation, you can introduce various types of pasta — such as elbow macaroni, wagon wheels, shells or thin noodles — for your youngster to layer along with the beans.

Streamers This is an exercise in crossing the midline of the body — reaching objects on the left side of the body with the right hand and on the right side with the left hand. It is an important skill, since reading and writing require this ability to move freely between the two sides. To make a streamer, tie a length of wide ribbon or plastic surveyor's tape (generally available at a low cost in hardware stores) to a short dowel. Show your child how to wave the streamer in the wind and trace large patterns in the air *(above)*, including designs that require her hand to reach across her body midline. After she has practiced with one hand, have her switch to the other.

Cutting edges Although some three-year-olds can pick up a pair of scissors and cut a sheet of paper in half with little apparent effort, many youngsters will require practice to develop this manipulative skill. To provide a precursor to cutting, you might show your youngster how to use tongs to pick up small objects, perhaps even making a game out of carrying the objects from one point to another. Alternatively, you can teach your child how to use spring-type clothespins on a clothesline. These activities help the child to develop the opposition movement of the fingers that must be mastered before cutting is possible.

Once your child is ready for scissors, give her a blunt-edged pair designed especially for children. In choosing scissors, be sure, too, to take into account which hand your child favors. If she seems to be left-handed, buy a left-handed pair of scissors; do not try to change her preference by forcing her to use right-handed scissors.

At first, you will want to teach your child how to cut strips of paper from the edges of the sheet. Later on, after she has had considerable practice cutting, you can show her how to snip along lines and how to cut large square and rectangular shapes from paper. ❖

Four to Five Years

Large-Muscle Control

- Walks down stairs alternating feet from step to step.

- Can stay balanced while walking backward several steps, with heels touching toes.

- Carries a cup of water several feet without spilling it.

- Stands on one foot for five seconds or more.

- Can hop for two or three yards on a single foot, either right or left.

- Gallops, skipping with one foot while taking walking steps with the other.

- Throws a ball overhand 12 or more feet.

- Catches a ball in hands with arms bent at the elbows.

- Turns sharp corners on a tricycle.

- Climbs ladders at the playground.

- Hangs from the top of a jungle gym.

70

Small-Muscle Control

- Can touch thumb to the tip of each finger in turn.

- Drops small objects, such as beads, into a small-necked bottle.

- Folds and creases paper vertically, horizontally and diagonally.

- Builds three steps with six blocks after being shown how.

- Cuts a straight line with scissors.

- Can slip paper clips onto the edges of two sheets of paper.

- Uses a pencil sharpener.

- Around the age of four, draws stick-figure people that feature heads, eyes and legs; by five, adds hair and fingers.

- Dresses independently, slipping on pull-up garments, zipping zippers, buttoning front buttons, buckling belts and lacing up shoes on the correct feet. May still need

a little help with pullover garments.

- Holds fork and spoon in a more grown-up fashion, using fingers instead of fist.

71

Large-Muscle Activities

like a statue and freeze in that position. Count to five, then tell him to assume a new shape. Continue to play in this manner for a while and, as you do, begin specifying the shapes you want to see — for example, stretched out, hunched up, crooked or relaxed. Finally, tell the child to run to the center of the room, jump up quickly and make a shape, then continue running to the opposite wall. The quick changes of running, stopping and starting again will enhance balance and agility.

Jumping hurdles As your child becomes more adept at jumping, you can help him refine this skill by setting up a course of low hurdles for him to hop over. Safe and simple hurdles may be constructed out of yardsticks or broomsticks laid atop sections of four-by-four-inch lumber, stacks of books or large cardboard building blocks standing on end. Start out by placing the bar at an angle, with one end on the floor and the other on the support, about 12 inches high. As your child's skill grows, place the other end of the dowel on a support also *(below)*. Do not attach the sticks to the supports. Simply lay them across the blocks, so that they will fall off if the child fails to clear a hurdle. Leave at least 10 to 12 feet between hurdles.

Through the loop This exercise promotes flexibility and balance. Begin by showing your child how you pass one loop through another when you tie his shoes. Then tell him you know a way that he can put his whole body through a loop. Have him bend over and clasp his fingers together to form a loop with his arms. Then tell him to step through the loop, one foot at a time *(above)*. If he succeeds, tell him to step back through the loop again.

Freeze Like many other good children's games, this one can be played by one youngster or several, and it requires no special equipment. Simply tell the players to move any way they wish, count to 10 and shout, "Freeze!" At that point the players must freeze in position and remain motionless until you release them. As the game progresses, specify how you want your players to move — whether crouching, running, leaping or hopping — as well as their speed and direction. Or ask them to move happily or sadly, or in pairs or bunches. Through the game, children discover the many ways that they can move, and they also improve their balance.

Jumping statues Similar to freeze is jumping statues, a game in which the child runs, jumps, quickly assumes a shape and then goes on running. As a warm-up, ask the youngster to make a shape

Hitting a ball Most preschoolers lack the refined eye-hand coordination needed to hit a pitched ball with a bat. But by suspending the ball on a piece of string, you can help your youngster enjoy some of the fun of playing baseball without the frustration of constantly missing.

Plastic balls are best for this purpose, but you can also use old socks rolled up into a ball. Hang the ball with a sturdy piece of twine from a rafter in the basement or from the branch of a tree. Let it dangle at about the height of the youngster's waist. Give him a plastic bat or the cardboard tube from a roll of wrapping paper and tell him to swing away.

Beanbags Beanbags are useful play equipment that can help in developing manipulative skills and in refining balance. Tossing beanbags at stairsteps, for example, will help improve your preschooler's muscle control. If you want, place rewards such as raisins, nuts or fruit on each step as an incentive *(below)*. Or you might assign a certain number of points for each step. To teach stability, challenge the child to drop a beanbag and then pick it up again without moving his feet. Then have him toss it a little farther away and stretch to get it back while keeping one foot planted on the floor. Other balancing games for your child include holding a beanbag on his outstretched arm or foot, or walking with one on his head, shoulder or hand. ❖

Bottle bowling This activity, which requires empty plastic soda bottles and a large rubber or plastic ball, can be great fun for you and your child, and it is also an excellent way to develop a preschooler's eye-hand coordination. Outline a bowling lane with masking tape on a smooth, uncarpeted floor. Then set up six to 10 empty two-liter bottles, with caps screwed on, at one end of the lane in a triangular pattern, like real bowling pins. Start your youngster about six or seven feet from the pins, showing him how to roll the ball to hit them *(above)*. At first, it may be all your child can do just to hit the bottles. But in time he will improve and you can move the starting line farther from the bottles.

Reaching higher Another jumping game that can be played either indoors or out involves leaping to touch strips of cloth suspended overhead. In addition to presenting an irresistible challenge, this game develops eye-hand coordination and physical strength. To set up this exercise, hang a variety of colored fabric streamers from the middle of the ceiling in a large room or from a rope tied between two trees outside. Make each target hang an inch or two higher than the one next to it, with the lowest about one foot above the child's head. If you like, attach small bells to the streamers as an auditory reward for successful leaps. Give the youngster room for a running start and have him attempt the lower targets first.

Small-Muscle Activities

pretend that the clothespin is talking to him. To enhance the appeal of this activity, draw a face on one side of the clothespin and invite your child to make up stories as he makes the doll "talk." Once he has shown that he can handle one clothespin, draw a face on a second one for his other hand and encourage him to use both to act out a simple scene.

Making more elaborate dolls out of push-on clothespins will also provide plenty of exercise for small fingers, though your youngster may need some help. Begin by assembling a few clothespins, some yarn, bits of fabric, pipe cleaners, ribbon or string, and glue. Then show your child how to turn the clothespins into dolls by twisting on pipe-cleaner arms, slipping fabric pants over the prongs of the clothespins and using other bits of cloth as shirts and dresses. A piece of ribbon or string will make a fine belt and frayed scraps of yarn will double as hair, glued on the heads of the clothespins. Finally, let the child draw the faces with a felt-tip marker.

Paper mosaics This rainy-day diversion will give your youngster plenty of practice manipulating small pieces of paper and will also foster creativity. White glue or paste, some construction paper and a few sheets of white paper are all that you need to get started. Let your child tear the construction paper into small pieces, while you outline his initials in thick block letters on a sheet of white paper. If you like, you can also draw one or two simple designs on other sheets. Once the tearing is completed, show the child how to smear the white space enclosed within the outlined initials or designs with glue or paste and then cover the sticky spaces with the torn bits of paper *(above)*. The youngster can create a mosaic effect if he alternates colors as he sets the paper bits in the glue.

Sign language Communicating with your child in sign language is another excellent way to promote manual dexterity. Buy a sign language guidebook and teach the youngster a few everyday expressions. These can then become your secret code that you can use to communicate with each other whenever appropriate. Each time you do, you will be giving the child's hand and wrist muscles a workout.

Clothespin people Playing with dolls made from clothespins — both the spring type and the old-fashioned push-on variety — can help develop your child's manual dexterity. Spring-type clothespins will exercise the youngster's pincer grasp. Give him a clothespin and show him how to pinch it open and closed. As you do,

Target practice Many children love to spray things with a toy water-pistol, and squirting a stream of water at a target can actually help improve a youngster's eye-hand coordination. If you prefer that your child not play with toy guns, simply substitute a well-rinsed squeeze bottle or spray-cleaner bottle for the water pistol.

To set up the practice range, use plastic or paper cups as targets and line them up on the front edge of the kitchen sink or outside on a step or ledge. Let your child take aim and fire at the targets. As his aim improves, you can add other lightweight unbreakable items as targets, balance several cups atop one another or dangle yogurt cup lids from a string.

Skelly This game was originally played outside on pavement that had been chalked with numbered squares. You can just as easily make it an indoor game by decorating a large piece of cardboard with brightly colored squares and making a deck of corresponding cards *(page 84)*. To begin play, each player is given a counter from a game of checkers. The object of the game is to flick the checker with the fingertip into the square indicated by the uppermost card of the accompanying deck. The player who gets the checker in the correct square on one try is allowed to continue until he has moved through every square on the board. If he misses the square or lands in the no man's land around the center square, then the next player takes a turn. This game will improve eye-hand coordination.

Marbles Shooting marbles is another time-honored childhood pastime that is particularly good for eye-hand coordination. To introduce your child to this activity, cut openings of varying widths along one side of a shoebox, then turn it upside down on the floor. Show the child how to roll or flick the marbles, aiming for the openings in the shoebox *(above)*.

Homemade puzzles Making simple puzzles will give your youngster an opportunity to practice the scissor skills he first started learning as a two-year-old. As always, the child should use only blunt-tipped scissors that are made for the hand he prefers. Do not force him to use right-handed scissors if you have observed that he does most things with his left hand.

As raw materials for puzzles, find brightly colored magazine covers, simple maps or expendable pieces of the child's own artwork. On the back of each picture draw cutting lines that are simple enough for your child to follow. Have him snip the puzzle pieces apart, then turn them all over and see whether he can put the puzzle back together.

Build a person Making people out of clay, using small household objects for the clothes, limbs and facial features, encourages creativity and develops finger dexterity. Before starting, gather a supply of such items as toothpicks, wooden ice-cream sticks, buttons, straws, beads and any other items you think might be appropriate, along with modeling clay or play dough *(pages 62-63)*. Then ask your child to use these materials to make a likeness of somebody he knows. Give him only as much help as he needs and encourage him to use his imagination. Later on, you might suggest that he use the same materials to build animals or anything else he dreams up.

Printing Printing is an activity that intrigues young children and one that promotes small-muscle control as well. It is even more fun when you make your own printing set, which can be done inexpensively using materials readily available in the kitchen or elsewhere around the house. To make a stamp pad, for example, pour any nontoxic paint into a shallow pan lined with a few folded paper towels, until the towels are well-soaked. Then cut a green pepper or cucumber in half to use as a printing block. Or cut a potato in half and carve a simple design, such as a triangle or square, on its cut face. Show your youngster how to coat the block with paint from the stamp pad and press it onto paper to make a design. As he gains skill, you can add to his supply of printing blocks, using apples, oranges, sponges, empty thread spools, leaves or keys. Just about anything that can be cut into an interesting design — and will not be harmed by the paint — can be used as a block.

Braiding Twisting and braiding yarn is a constructive exercise for small fingers. At first, make the task as easy as possible by using just two thick strands of yarn attached at one end to a doorknob *(below)*. Let the child twist the strands around each other for as long as he likes. Later, introduce a third length of yarn to the process and teach him the traditional technique of braiding, in which you alternate from right to left, turning the outside strands over the center one, each time creating a new center strand. If the braided yarn is long enough, you can tie a knot at each end and let your child use it as a belt. ❖

Five to Six Years

Large-Muscle Control

- Marches to music, approximately following the beat.

- Can touch fingertips to toes without bending at the knees.

- Runs fluidly and seldom falls. Sprints 35 yards in 10 seconds or less.

- Balances on either foot for 10 seconds.

- Hops forward four to eight times consecutively on either foot.

- Can swing either leg back and forth without losing balance.

- Bounces a tennis ball with one hand and catches it with two hands.

- Steps up to a large ball and then kicks it without stopping.

- Skips on alternate feet.

- Stands balanced on tiptoes with hands placed on hips.

- Jumps backward.

- Can walk backward heel to toe along a marked line.

Small-Muscle Control

- Shapes recognizable objects out of clay.

- Winds thread onto a spool.

- Can gather tissue paper into a crumpled ball with one hand.

- Cuts out squares with scissors from construction paper.

- Puts a folded letter into an envelope.

- Fits holed paper into a ring binder.

- Distinguishes own right from left side. Handedness is well established.

- Can thread a needle with a large eye.

- Sews plastic-tipped laces through holes punched through cards.

- Can knot a shoelace or a length of yarn around a pencil.

- Puts on sweaters and pullover shirts independently.

- Washes and dries hands and face without getting clothing wet.

- Spreads peanut butter and jelly on bread with a table knife.

Large-Muscle Activities

Points This versatile activity is fun for parent and child alone, and it can also be played with a group of children. The idea of the game is to have the child balance on one or more points — hands, fingers, elbows, head, bottom, knees, heels, toes or feet. Start the game by challenging her to balance on two points and see what combinations she chooses; if she needs help getting started, suggest a hand-and-foot balance or a knee-and-elbow combination to begin. Then try one-point and three-point balancing. Later on, you can vary the activity by challenging her to shift from a three-point balance to two points, or from four points to three, without falling over.

Animal walks By the time they are five, most children are familiar with some of the ways in which animals move and will usually need little coaxing to hop around like bunnies or frogs *(below)* or lumber along like some larger beast. Such activities are good exercises for developing a youngster's locomotor skills and balance; they also challenge her young imagination. Try asking your preschooler to walk like a bear, leap like a kangaroo or gallop like a horse. You might also request that she stand like a stork, waddle like a seal or crawl like a caterpillar. Think of variations that your own child would know how to perform.

Hopscotch Hopscotch is a classic children's game that is most fun when played by at least two children. Before starting, you will need to chalk a hopscotch grid outside on the walk or driveway. There are several variations of the hopscotch grid; teach your child the one that you remember best from childhood or use the design on page 85. Traditionally, the game is played with a stone marker tossed from square to square within the grid while standing at the base line or rest area. Stones tend to bounce, however, and five-year-olds will find it less frustrating if they use a beanbag or an old set of keys for the marker.

   The objective of the game is for the player to throw her marker into each square of the grid in sequence, each time hopping through the grid without stepping on any lines *(above)*. In some parts of the grid the child hops on one foot; in others she must land with both feet on the ground. Moving in one direction through the grid, the player hops over the square containing her marker; on the return trip she must bend over to retrieve the marker. A player does not get to begin a new turn until she successfully tosses the marker within the lines of the next numbered square. If she should fail to get the marker in the proper square, or if she steps on a line or loses her balance and puts her other foot on the ground at any point during her turn, the play then passes to the next player. Hopscotch is an excellent way to develop throwing, balancing and hopping skills.

Coffee-can stilts Coffee-can stilts, which are fashioned from empty coffee cans and rope *(page 85)*, challenge a youngster's stability by raising her center of gravity and making balancing more difficult. Once up on the stilts *(opposite, left)*, your child should practice walking in all di-

rections — forward, backward and sideways. As
she grows more confident, let her try stepping over low objects.

With two or more children, you can organize stilt-walking races across the room. Or try
this variation: Place a stack of coins on a
shelf that is barely within the child's reach
while she is up on the stilts. Have her pick
up one coin and cross the room on the stilts to
deposit it in a container before returning
for another coin. Continue the exercise until
she gets all the coins in the container.

Mirrors Ask your child to mirror every move you
make. Doing so requires considerable concentration on the part of the youngster, but the
rewards are enhanced muscle control, flexibility and eye-hand coordination, and greater
awareness of how her body moves.

Have the child stand directly in front of
you, a few paces away. Move just one part of
your body at first and keep your movements very slow. Encourage her to watch carefully: She should be trying to imitate your
actions almost as soon as you make them. Once
she understands the game, you can begin to
move in more complex ways, eventually moving your entire body. After a while, reverse
roles and let your child lead.

Acrobatics Every child enjoys a circus, and given a few
props and a little imagination, you can stage
your own three-ring spectacle at home, featuring activities designed to promote strength,
balance and agility. You can double as the acro-
bat's assistant and the ringmaster, announc-
ing each act with simulated drum roll and
trumpet fanfares. The acrobatics can include any or all of the following, depending on
your youngster's abilities and interests. For
safety reasons, these activities should be performed on a mat or a carpet.

Airplane: To turn your child into an airplane,
lie flat on your back with your knees against
your chest, while the youngster stands facing
you. Have her lean on her tummy against
the soles of your feet, stretching her hands forward. Take hold of her hands and gently lift
her into the air with your feet. If you can, balance her in midair while she holds her arms
out like airplane wings.

Bareback rider: Carry your child around
the room piggyback, then drop to your hands
and knees and let the youngster pretend to
be a bareback rider.

Wheelbarrow: Have the youngster lie on
her tummy on the floor. Take hold of her legs
just above the ankles and let her walk for-

ward on her hands as you guide the human
wheelbarrow *(above).* If your child has
trouble supporting herself, you should hold her
at her knees instead.

Headstand: Have your child kneel with her
hands flat on the floor in front of her knees,
fingers spread apart. Then tell her to lower her
head to the mat so that her head and hands
form the three points of a triangle. Help her to
straighten her legs and walk her feet forward toward her hands. Ease her legs into the
air, supporting her ankles with your hands.

Balance beam: Let your youngster test her balancing skills with the use of a homemade
balance beam — which is nothing more than an
eight-foot length of two-by-four lumber,
sanded around the edges and placed on the
ground or floor. She can make believe the
board is a high wire, for example, and walk forward and backward across it or edge along
it sideways. As she becomes more adept at it,
have her try to cross the beam balanced on
her heels or tiptoes, or walk across with a beanbag resting on her forehead or with a wand
balanced in one hand.

Scoops A five-year-old can use a scoop made from an
empty plastic bleach or milk container
(page 84) to practice throwing and catching.
Show the child how to toss a rubber ball
with the scoop, swinging it underhand, overhand and sidearm. Using your hands or another scoop, play catch with the child, flinging
the ball back and forth. For solitary play,
you can have the youngster throw the ball at a
wall and try to catch it herself on the re-
bound. Scoops can also be used to play modi-
fied versions of volleyball or dodge ball. ⋰

79

Small-Muscle Activities

Jacks Like tiddlywinks, jacks is a game that requires a great deal of eye-hand coordination and finger dexterity. To get your child started, you can buy a set of jacks at most toy or variety stores, although you can easily substitute pebbles of relatively equal size and a small, high-bouncing ball.

Before beginning, give your youngster a brief explanation of the game and its rules, along with a demonstration. First, scatter six jacks on the playing surface. Show her how to toss the ball upward *(below)* and, using the same hand, how to scoop up one of the jacks, then catch the ball after it has bounced only once. She must transfer the jack to her other hand and then repeat the sequence, again and again, one jack at a time. Remind her that the ball can bounce only once, that it must

Lacing and threading Here are activities that will give your youngster some practice in lacing and threading. You will need an old pair of shoes, laces, beads, cardboard, a hole puncher and some construction paper. Begin by punching a few holes into a piece of cardboard. Show your youngster how to thread a shoelace through the holes, perhaps having her add a few beads to the lace every now and then. As soon as your child masters this lacing skill, you can let her try the real thing, giving her a shoe and helping her to string a lace through the eyelets.

Having mastered lacing, your child can try the similar but more artistic task of weaving paper strips through a paper frame *(above)*. Prepare the frame beforehand by making several rows of horizontal or vertical slits about one and one half inches wide on a sheet of construction paper, leaving the border uncut on all sides. Cut one-inch-wide strips of paper of different colors and teach your preschooler how to weave the strips through the slits on the paper frame.

Tiddlywinks A set of tiddlywinks can be purchased inexpensively in a toy store or can be made at home using an empty margarine tub or four connecting sections of an egg carton as a cup, and a number of flat buttons, washers or coins as disks. To play, take one disk and press it down on the edge of a second disk, flipping the second disk forward into the cup. When a player misses the cup, the turn passes to the next player. The one who gets the most tiddlywinks into the cup wins.

be caught in the same hand that picked up the jacks, and that it is against the rules to touch any jack other than the one she is trying to scoop up. This is the first round, known as onesies. Once she has mastered this stage, your youngster can go on to twosies, threesies, foursies and so on, in each case picking up the appropriate number of jacks after tossing the ball.

Catch the cup Snaring a cup on the end of a stick challenges a child's eye-hand coordination and agility. To make the equipment for this activity,

you need a dowel, string and a yogurt cup *(page 85)*. Have your youngster hold one end of the dowel and, swinging her arm forward, flip the cup upward *(above)*. Then, keeping her eye on the cup, the child should position the dowel so that the cup will land on top of it.

Pipe-cleaner sculpture Pipe cleaners traditionally have been used for making minisculptures — a simple and inexpensive activity that fosters manual dexterity as well as creativity. Buy pipe cleaners in different colors and show your youngster how to shape them to form little people or other objects, twisting onto the first pipe cleaner a second or third one when necessary to complete a sculpture. After people, she might want to try making animals, trees, cars and houses. Encourage her to play with her new creations or use them to tell a story.

Junior golf In preparation for making a miniature golf course, save up a number of empty bleach bottles, clean them well and use a felt-tip marker to draw a large number on each bottle. Pour a little sand into the bottles to weigh them down, then screw on the caps. To play, lay out a course by setting the bottles around the yard. Give your preschooler a rubber or plastic ball and a broomstick, plastic bat or croquet mallet to use as a golf club. She could also use a putter. Show her how to hit the ball toward each target in succession. As she does, call out the number of the one she is aiming for and count the number of strokes she takes to hit the ball so that it strikes the side of the bottle.

Hot potato Hot potato is best played with a large group of children, and parents will have fun joining in, too. The players sit in a circle, and on the command "Go," they begin to pass a potato or small ball around the circle until they are told to stop. The player who is caught holding the hot potato at this moment is out, and the game then continues until only two players are left. As an alternative to being declared out, which can be upsetting to some children, you can use a point system, assigning one point to the person left holding the hot potato in each round. As soon as any player has three points, she must sit in the center of the circle for one turn, or she must perform some stunt for the group.

Potato carry This delightful game rewards small-muscle strength and balance. All your child needs is a small potato and a soup spoon large enough to hold it. Give your child the spoon and balance the potato in its bowl. Then, standing about six feet away from her, tell her to walk to you while carrying the potato with the spoon *(below)*. As your youngster grows more confident in the activity, you can vary the game by standing farther away or by having the child run, squat, walk sideways or backward, or weave from side to side without dropping the potato. ❖

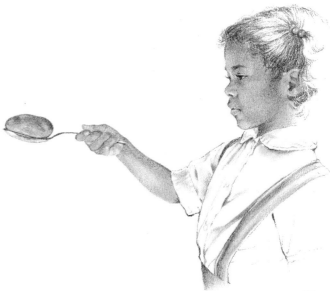

Equipment for Activities

Children often enjoy an activity more when they can take part in buying or making the equipment for it. Guidelines for choosing basic balls and blocks appear below. Many other items used for the large- and small-muscle exercises in this section of the book can easily be made at home; simple instructions for several of them are given here.

Balls

Select balls that are suited to the skills you wish to focus on: Small hands require small balls for successful throwing, while larger balls, about nine inches in diameter, are easier for young children to catch. Regulation sports equipment such as basketballs and footballs are too hard and heavy for the very young. Instead, choose balls made of soft, lightweight material such as foam or plastic; this will minimize the risk of injury and also reduce the chance that your youngster will become fearful of balls thrown her way.

Blocks

Building blocks — whether bought at the toy store or home-made from grocery bags stuffed with newspaper *(page 54)* — can provide young children with hours of creative play, as well as valuable exercise for muscles large and small. Toddlers can stack and sort blocks; older children can create designs on the floor, lay roadways and bridges, and build towers, castles and more fanciful structures. Children of any age take plea-sure in knocking them down.

A set of blocks made up of a wide variety of shapes — in-cluding arches, cylinders and triangles — allows more opportu-

nity for experimentation than a set consisting only of cubes. Both plain and colored blocks have advantages: Those made of uncolored natural wood effectively stimulate a child's spatial creativity, while blocks painted in vivid primary hues add the creative dimension of color to block play.

It is a good idea to limit your toddler to about eight blocks at first, when she is only beginning to develop her manipulative skills. You can get her started by showing her how to stack them. As she becomes more skilled with her hands, you can add more blocks of varying shapes and sizes.

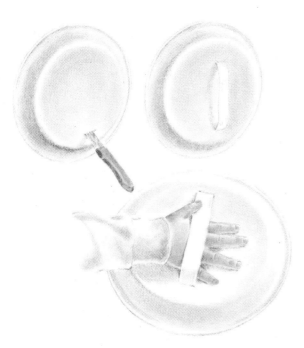

Palm Paddles
- To make each of the palm paddles, use one plastic or foam plate or several paper plates glued together or taped together around the edges.

- Cut two 2-inch slits about 5 inches apart in each of the plates, as illustrated above.

- Thread one end of a 10-inch-long strip of 1-inch-wide waistband elastic through one of the slits, then thread the other end through the second slit.

- Bring the ends of the elastic together behind the plate and fasten them with tape, staples or thread. Cover any exposed staples with tape to prevent injury.

Rings and Hooks
- Attach half a dozen self-adhesive hooks to one side of a 12-by-12-inch square of cardboard, making two rows of three hooks each, as shown below.

- For rings to hang on the hooks, use canning jar rings or cut the rings from the plastic tops of margarine tubs, potato-chip cans or instant baby-food containers.

- Rings can also be made by tracing concentric circles, one slightly smaller than the other, on a sheet of heavy cardboard, and then using scissors to cut them out.

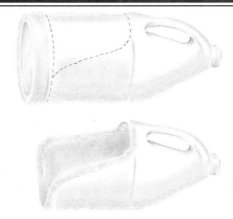

Scoops

- For each scoop, cut the bottom from an empty half-gallon plastic bleach or milk bottle, as indicated above.

- Cut an opening that starts below the handle and slants down toward the open bottom of the bottle.

- Cover all exposed edges of the bottle with heavy-duty tape to prevent accidental scrapes.

Beanbags

- Cut old pieces of fabric into a variety of shapes and sizes: circles, squares, rectangles, diamonds and triangles. There should be two matching pieces of fabric for each beanbag.

- Place two matching shapes together, with the right surfaces of the fabric facing inward, and then stitch the shapes together about ¼ inch from the edges, leaving an inch-long opening along one side.

- Turn the beanbag shell inside out by pushing the stitched edges through the opening, until the right surfaces of the fabric are facing outward.

- Fill the shell with dried beans or corn, rice or Styrofoam® chips, then hand-sew the opening closed.

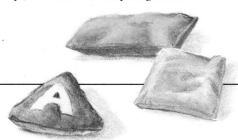

Skelly Board

- Cut a 24-by-24-inch square of cardboard. With a felt-tip marker, draw a pattern of squares on the cardboard similar to the pattern pictured below. Each of the squares should be about 4 inches square.

- Decorate the squares with shapes such as diamonds, circles and triangles or with sketches of simple objects such as flowers or teddy bears.

- Make a deck of 4-inch-square cardboard cards, each bearing a duplicate of a shape or symbol drawn on the large cardboard square. Make sure that you have a card to match each of the shapes on the skelly board.

- Use checkers for tokens.

Catch the Cup

- Punch a small hole in the center of the bottom of an empty yogurt cup.

- Make a knot at one end of a length of string and, starting from the bottom exterior of the yogurt container, draw the other end of the string through the punched hole and through the interior of the cup, as illustrated below.

- With heavy-duty tape, attach the unknotted end of the string about 2 inches from one end of an 8-inch long dowel. Hold the dowel at the end closest to the string and point it downward. Adjust the length of the string so that the open end of the yogurt cup dangles an inch from the lower end of the dowel when it is held this way.

Coffee-Can Stilts

- Turn an empty coffee can upside down and, with a can opener, punch a hole in the side of the can near the bottom; then punch a second hole on the other side, opposite the first. Cover exposed interior metal edges with heavy-duty tape.

- Cut two lengths of rope, each one measuring twice the distance from your youngster's waist to his feet.

- Thread one length of rope through the holes in one can and tie the rope ends together securely to form a large loop, as shown at top right. Thread the second rope through the other coffee can and tie it.

- Put the plastic lids back on the cans to save wear and tear on your carpets and floors and to cut down on noise.

Hopscotch

- With chalk, draw on the sidewalk or driveway a pattern of 12-inch squares and 12-by-24-inch rectangles, rounding each end with a semicircle similar to that pictured below.

- Number the boxes from one through eight.

- For tokens, use flat pebbles, beanbags or keys.

3 Speech and Language

Few experiences light the face of a toddler with such shining joy as her early successes in talking — even when the listener is a stuffed toy lamb, even when the word is childish jargon like "baa-sheep." Learning to talk is a thrill for a child. At last she is beginning to break the secret code by which the people around her communicate. As her vocabulary increases, she brims with the confidence of her new power. She can demand more juice. She can ask where her dolly is. And when something displeases her, she can say "No!"

But language is more than a key to the world that surrounds her. It also gives her new access to and more control over her own mind. With words she can bring order and shape to her thoughts — at first by speaking aloud to herself, later by constructing mental sentences that are never spoken.

Learning how to talk and acquiring increasingly complex language skills are crucial to the future well-being of a growing child. The process at times seems miraculous and mysterious: It is true that there are some aspects of it that even the experts do not fully understand. But enough is known to enable parents to keep track of a child's progress in this essential growth area and to alert them to signs that the youngster might need help with a speech- or language-development problem.

The Uses of Language

Your child is born with an urgent need to communicate, and in the nine to 14 months before he utters his first meaningful words, he spends considerable time exploring ways to accomplish his goal. Bit by bit he comes to an unconscious understanding that the sounds he produces are valuable tools for getting messages across and that the more distinctive his utterances, the better he is able to get what he is after. He first develops special cries for different problems, later begins to babble syllable-like noises and finally speaks real words. The praise and excitement of his parents as he progresses through these steps increase the frequency of his efforts, but the general developmental path that he follows seems to be set by nature.

As he relates the events of a television show, a four-year-old's animated facial expressions give extra meaning to his words. The combination of visible expressions and gestures with language makes what he says more interesting to his listeners. The attention that others give his story will reinforce his sense of self-worth.

Talking to others

Once a child experiences the thrill of verbal communication, he discovers that language has a great many uses. The most prominent use is in conversing with others — what child-language specialists call socialized speech. Those authorities have defined at least 10 different ways in which a child uses socialized speech. Among the earliest uses are acknowledgments of others and their comings and goings ("Hi" and "Bye-bye"), making requests and protests ("Gimme nana," and "No!"), and telling others what to do ("Watch me."). As time goes on he will also use speech to play games ("Peekaboo!"), express feelings and judgments ("I love you."), ask questions ("Where moon?"), give information ("that big airplane"), make promises ("I be good.") and invent poetic word plays for their own sake ("Mommy is pretty and loves the kitty."). Last, he will use socialized speech to recall past experiences and predict future ones: "I went to store," or "I not be scared next time."

Talking to oneself

Although communication is the first goal of speech development, language also serves a critical role in a young child's management of herself and ultimately in her emotional and intellectual growth. Sometimes termed private or self-directed speech, this broad category consists of conversations the child carries on with herself. In the beginning she talks aloud, but as a child gets older and more self-conscious, an increasing amount of this private guidance goes on silently.

The most frequently observed forms of private speech, particularly among very young children, are language play and language practice, in which the child produces sing-song sounds and phrases when she is all alone. Sometimes the activity is purely for her own entertainment. She gets a kind of sensual pleasure from making and hearing sounds. She may invent alliterative phrases by putting a uniform first letter or last letter on a series of words: "Tommy tickle tummy, Dommy dickle dummy...." She may pretend to read to herself, using nonsense words if she does not yet know real ones. And at other times — especially when her solitary chattering has a clearly recognizable content, such as counting out "one, two, three, four" — the child may be drilling herself in useful information.

Other functions of private speech Children also use self-directed speech to sharpen their understanding of ideas and to make the relationships between ideas more explicit. A youngster may examine two dolls and say to herself: "These same? No, this doll bigger. This doll mommy. That doll little girl doll." The adult does much the same when confronted with something unfamiliar, though usually silently.

Other related functions of private speech are self-guidance and the child's assessment of her own self-image. A three-year-old at work on a sand castle might say to herself: "I'm gonna make this tower tall. Find a big bucket and fill it to the top. Then I turn it over and — whop! — my tower is the biggest in the world!" She is not only verbally directing herself in the task at hand, but she is building her confidence that she will succeed, reinforcing her image of herself as a competent person. In the same way, a child who is about to go where she has been told not to may interrupt herself with, "No-no. No open door. No stairs. Fall." She is using private speech to become her own authoritative parent. Avoidance is another function of private speech. You will recognize it in the steady stream of chatter that comes from the youngster who hopes that talking will forestall some anticipated punishment or who wants to delay going to sleep.

Language into conversation Children begin learning how to hold a conversation long before they master their first words, perhaps as early as eight or nine weeks of age, with what has been called conversation-related behavior. A baby fixes his gaze on his parent's face and enters into an exchange of cooing noises and other vocalizations with the adult, the two of them taking turns listening and making sounds in their playful game. By the time the child reaches 10 months or a year, he is ready to attempt something closer to true conversation, which can be defined as verbal communication between two people who have each other's listening attention, who take turns in talking, who pursue a common subject and who advance the dialogue with each turn-taking by alternately adding new bits of information.

A child of about 18 months may be fairly adept at waiting his turn, though an urgent need to get an idea across sometimes overrides his self-restraint. At this age, however, the child may have a hard time consistently coming up with responses that are relevant to the subject being discussed. Often his contribution will be either a repetition of something the other speaker has said or an unrelated statement. When he does respond appropriately, the remark usually comes after some delay, because his thinking and his word retrieval skills are still relatively slow. But between his second and third birthdays a child's language skills usually improve enough for him to use conversation as a pleasurable form of self-expression and social exchange. By the time he is old enough for school, he probably will be more than able to keep up his end of discussions and may show a good deal of verbal playfulness and humor.

Parents' roles in encouraging language development

Almost from birth children pay attention to language. They notice how their parents' mouths move when producing sounds. They soon can distinguish between some sounds, and they read the moods and intentions of people speaking to them. As they attend to the language that accompanies routine activities such as baths and meals, and hear words and phrases repeated in the games that adults and siblings play with them, young children develop a surprising understanding of language. This happens months before they begin to speak recognizable words.

Parents who want to facilitate their young child's language development should provide a responsive and rich verbal environment from the start. Whenever you are together with your infant — at bathtime or feeding time, for instance — take the opportunity for gentle, unhurried talk and verbal play. Listen carefully so that you can build on what she is interested in. If the child does not talk yet, listen to the sounds she makes and respond to them, taking turns making babbling noises. Name objects and activities — "water," "wash," "bottle" — that she takes a special interest in and repeat the

A two-year-old chatters about untying her shoe as she tries to guide herself through the process. When the youngster is older, she may recite instructions to herself mentally.

words whenever she again experiences those things. Read or recite nursery rhymes to her again and again, so that she learns to anticipate familiar sounds and rhymes.

Adapt your delivery to hold your child's attention. Face her, so that she can watch the way you use your mouth to form sounds. (At the age of around seven months a baby typically begins to pay more attention to her mother's mouth than to her eyes, indicating that she is becoming interested in how to talk.) Pronounce words clearly and precisely, use short words and simple sentences, and stick to the present tense. Speak slowly and repeat important words and phrases to make a stronger impression. Use gestures and facial expressions that help to clarify meaning. When you say "This soup is so good," put the bowl in front of the baby, smile broadly and lick your lips with pleasure as you raise the spoon.

Also use gestures when you share a familiar picture book, pointing out the picture of the chair, dog, moon and so on, and then asking your child to do the same as you repeat the words slowly. Follow her lead. Stop when her interest flags. Keep your tone light and your expectations low, so that she never feels pressured. Resist impulses to correct too often. No one is more eager to become an accomplished talker than your child. And with plenty of love and encouragement, she will get there in her own good time. When she does learn to talk, keep the conversations going at an increasing level of sophistication, introducing new words and sentence forms as quickly as she seems interested in absorbing them. ❖

The story this three-year-old is telling her mother is important, but so are the conversational proprieties that are being reinforced by practice: politeness of tone, taking turns, making requests and responding to them.

A five-year-old boy shares a secret with a friend, then answers her question by explaining how his sole separated from his shoe. As children grow older, they become more adept at initiating and maintaining conversation with their peers and at conveying information about physical events.

Origins of Language Skill

It is clear that toddlers increase their vocabularies by listening to other people speak and by imitating what they hear. What is not clear is how they move on so quickly and easily to constructing complete, meaningful sentences, which are far more than just strings of independent words. How is it that a child as young as three, for example, is able to conjugate verbs, form plurals and possessives, and arrange words in sequence to tell the listener whether the sentence is a question, a declaration or a command — all without benefit of a single formal lesson in grammar?

Environmental influences At one time most psychologists tended to credit environmental conditioning for this language skill. They believed that grammatical development was a matter of children's imitating what they heard. After all, a youngster obviously is encouraged to use language correctly by a subtle process of reward and reinforcement. When a child says something in a way that others can understand and respond to appropriately, he experiences satisfaction and will try to express himself in the same manner again. But when he speaks in a form that is somehow incorrect — using the wrong word sequence or intonation or verb tense, for instance — he may be misunderstood, and his needs may not be fulfilled. Naturally he will gradually learn to abandon that form in favor of one that works better. This is why children who get relatively little verbal nurturing — fewer opportunities to listen to or practice talking with other people — may acquire language skills more slowly than those who are exposed to plenty of conversational give and take.

But imitation and reward alone do not explain the extraordinarily rapid acquisition of language that most children exhibit. If they could do no more than imitate what grownups say, then their own speech would consist of patched-together pieces of sentences they had heard. Yet, as every parent knows, children generate language of infinite variety with unique word combinations and sentences all their own. And if youngsters relied entirely upon praise and reinforcement to stir them to speak, they would not engage in private discussions with themselves, their dolls and the pet puppy, all of which they do regularly.

Biological factors For these and other reasons, most psycholinguists agree nowadays that language development is not all a result of nurture, that there is also some biological basis for a child's ability to employ our complex system of verbal communication. One possibility is that children are born with an innate capacity for language. This theory suggests that babies arrive "prewired" with highly spe-

How Speech Is Produced

Speech is one of the most complicated physical actions that the human brain directs. Speech centers in the brain coordinate hundreds of specialized muscles in the chest, throat and mouth to produce the multiplicity of sounds that constitute spoken language. While the entire respiratory system is involved in this process, the larynx, tongue, lips and palate perform the crucial roles.

Muscles in the chest force a flow of air from the lungs. The expelled air passes through the larynx, which is the top section of the windpipe containing the vocal cords. Through the workings of muscles and cartilage, the vocal cords have a wide range of motion: They are open and relaxed for breathing and for unvoiced consonant sounds such as *f* and *s (inset, top)*. For the voiced consonants and all vowels, the cords are held more tightly closed and vibrate as air passes over them *(inset, bottom)*. High and low pitch are determined by the frequency of vocal cord vibrations.

The various sounds of speech are produced by movements of the tongue, palate, lips and teeth. Consonant sounds such as *d* or *t* are made by cutting off the flow of air from the larynx by bringing together the tongue and palate. For vowel sounds, air flows freely out of the mouth and the sound is determined by the positions of the tongue, teeth and lips.

Success in speaking depends not only on learning to control tongue, teeth and lips, but also on waiting for them to develop. A newborn's tongue fills most of his mouth and cannot be manipulated to form consonants until the mouth cavity grows large enough. Sounds take on the distinctive qualities of an individual voice by resonating within the throat, mouth and nose prior to leaving the mouth. In general, the larger these cavities, the deeper the voice.

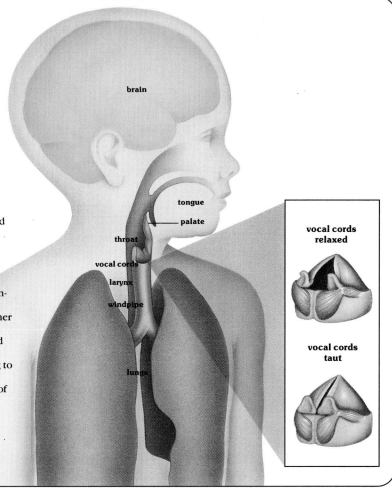

brain

tongue

palate

throat

vocal cords

larynx

windpipe

lungs

vocal cords relaxed

vocal cords taut

cialized neurological circuits in the brain that are devoted solely to verbal communication. These circuits, it is argued, enable youngsters to know by instinct certain fundamental rules of grammar that govern the structure of all language and to memorize the vocabulary necessary for human speech.

Another possibility is that language development is shaped by general cognitive development, itself a matter of genetic inheritance and the biological maturing process. Advances in cognitive development open the way to successively higher stages of language acquisition. If this is so, then each child develops language skills at a rate that is linked to her expanding memory and growing ability to think in the abstract. According to this point of view, a child can make full use of her verbal environment, however rich it may be, only when her brain has developed enough to perceive the principles underlying language and put them into practice. Although the exact nature of the biological factors involved are not yet known, the progressive stages of language-skill development are fairly well mapped out, as is explained on the following pages. ∴

A Guide to Progress in Speaking

For many parents a child's learning to talk is a vaguely understood process, though an exciting one. They thrill to the first clear word or words and eagerly note early additions to the tot's vocabulary. But as the child's control of language gradually improves, her parents may become so used to her chattering that they barely notice, or do not recognize, significant milestones in her progress toward fluency. One day they suddenly realize that she is conversing in adult-style sentences and wonder just how, and maybe even exactly when, she acquired that skill.

Language development is not actually the random process that those parents mistakenly take it to be. The ability to talk usually evolves in an orderly fashion, although the pace differs from child to child. If you know what to look for — or, rather, what to listen for — you can track your child's development. Knowing what advances to anticipate, and approximately when, makes the whole experience more memorably pleasurable for parents. It may also occasionally enable you to subtly ease the child's way to a developmental milestone.

The following pages chart the normal course of language development, from the first words at around one year of age to the fluency displayed by most five-year-olds. The time frames, of course, are only approximate, because there are great variations in the rate of normal developments. If you believe that your youngster may have a speech or language-development problem, see pages 106-107.

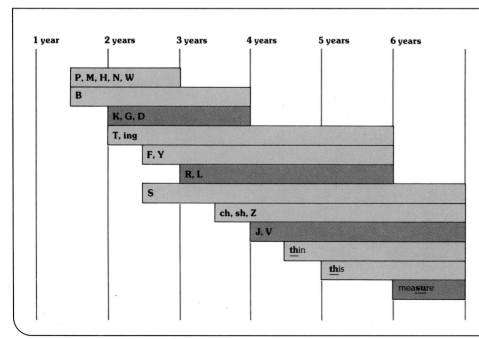

Learning to Articulate the Consonant Sounds

The chart at left shows the sequence in which children normally acquire the use of the consonant sounds, which are harder to produce than the vowel sounds that typify baby talk. The majority of children do not master the full range of spoken consonant sounds until after the age of six, and some youngsters do not perfect the last of them — sounds such as s and th — until they are seven or older. For each consonant sound shown on the chart, a bar begins where 50 percent of children can articulate that sound in any position within a word. The bar ends at the point where 90 percent of all children have mastered the sound.

The prespeech year A baby's speech development begins long before he can actually talk. It starts with his acute hearing: He can distinguish the sound of a voice from other noises at birth, probably even earlier. A typical infant begins to make vowel sounds between a month and two months of age. This cooing, as it is known, is important, since it enables a baby to rehearse some 90 percent of all the vowel sounds he will need later. Around the sixth month the child enters the babbling phase, using consonant-vowel combinations as well as duplicate syllables, such as "ba-ba" and "ma-ma." Two months later the child adds intonation — raising and lowering the pitch of his voice — and by around 10 months, his babbling so closely mimics the tones and syllables of normal speech that a proud parent can almost imagine the child is talking, but in a foreign language.

Meanwhile, when dealing with the infant, mothers, fathers and even siblings as young as four unconsciously modify their normal speech in ways that encourage him to talk. These adaptations, which researchers call "Motherese," include speaking more slowly, speaking in a higher pitch with exaggerated variations in intonation and using a more restricted vocabulary in shorter, simpler sentences. Parents continue to adapt their speech as the child's language abilities mature, gently nudging him along toward greater proficiency. He in turn gives clues to his readiness by his attention, his responsiveness, and eventually by his desire to say something himself. ∴

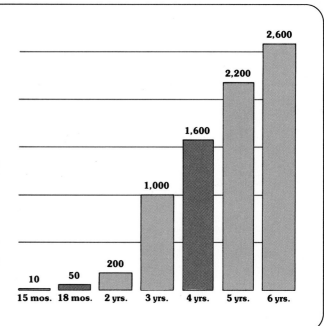

The Rate of Vocabulary Growth

As children begin to use a wider variety of sounds, they are better able to perceive the differences in the words spoken around them. This contributes to an extraordinarily rapid growth in vocabulary. The chart at right shows the average expansion in spoken vocabulary between the ages of 15 months and six years. At all stages, however, the vocabulary that a child comprehends exceeds the vocabulary that he uses in speech — at some points by a ratio of as much as 5 to 1. Thus, at the time a youngster has a spoken vocabulary of 10 words, he may understand 50. By the age of six the number of words comprehended may total more than 12,000.

15 mos.	18 mos.	2 yrs.	3 yrs.	4 yrs.	5 yrs.	6 yrs.
10	50	200	1,000	1,600	2,200	2,600

One to Two Years

Sometime around their first birthday, most toddlers probably will be saying "mama" and "dada" and perhaps half a dozen other words, although it is neither unusual nor alarming for a child not to speak until as much as six months later. Some babble until 18 months and only then begin acquiring words. But they understand better than they speak: At the same time that your youngster starts to use his first five to 10 words, he may well be able to comprehend and act on as many as three dozen others that you say to him.

A child often invents his own first words, which linguists term expressive jargon. Parents and other caregivers recognize them as words because the child uses a particular combination of sounds again and again in the same context, often accompanied by pointing and other gestures. Some of these made-up words are based on imperfect imitations of adult speech — "nana" for banana, "ta-ta" for thank you. Some come from the imitation of a sound associated with the object — "rhum-rhum" for car, "moo" for cow, "whoo-ooo" for an electric fan. Still others are combinations of tongue clicks, straining sounds, whines, grunts and "aaahs" used with consistency to express such notions as "give me" or "look," for which the youngster has not yet acquired conventional words.

Typical early words: nouns

First spoken words are often nouns naming people and objects that interest the child most. Naturally these include — in addition to his parents — things that move, that taste good, that make sounds he likes to hear and that he can directly act on and experience. Dog, cat, ball, juice, truck and an older sibling are likely to be high on his list of favorite attractions, although the toddler's own invented names for them might be indecipherable to people outside his immediate circle. At the same time, the youngster may understand such words as "house," "table" and "tree," but because they describe parts of the background environment, he does not find the words inviting enough to try to master in his own speech.

Demand words

Instead of building a repertoire of nouns, some children who are just beginning to talk concentrate on what can be termed interpersonal expressions, which include verbs and other non-noun words. Interpersonal expressions are words that convey a demand or a need or that serve to acknowledge a relationship of awareness between the child and the person he is addressing. The greeting "hi," which is an early favorite with many toddlers, is an expression serving the latter purpose. "Up," meaning "pick me up," and "stop" (or more likely, "top," from a new talker), meaning just what it says, are common examples of demand words.

Studies have found that while some children who are learning to talk start by collecting nouns and others begin by working on interpersonal expressions, no long-term difference results. Within a matter of months both groups have acquired a balance of both kinds of words.

Most of the beginning talker's words are one-syllable and start with consonants formed at the front of the mouth, such as *p, b, d, t, m* or *n.* The occasional two-syllable words, "mama" and "dada" included, are typically what linguists call reduplicating words, in which the second syllable echoes the first: "Bye-bye" and "night-night" are other examples.

Stretching small vocabularies

Even in this first phase of speech, children use their limited vocabularies not only to name things but to express sentence-like ideas. When the child brings a favorite box to her father and says "Open," she is saying, in effect, "Open this box for me." When she points to her mother's eyeglasses lying on the table and says "Mama," her family clearly understands that she means "These glasses belong to my mother." Sometimes the meaning is not so clear. When she sees a car drive by and says "Bye-bye," she may be trying to indicate that the moving vehicle takes people places or that she wants to go for a ride or that her daddy is gone in his car and she misses him. When she says "No," however, there is rarely any doubt that she is rejecting the food, bath, game, shoe or toy being offered.

Sometimes a child stretches the effectiveness of a limited vocabulary by a technique that is known to language researchers as overextension. The youngster uses a single word to cover a variety of objects, people or activities in which she notes some common shape, size, sound, texture or movement. For a brief time, all men may be called "Daddy," all moving vehicles "car," everything to drink "juice," all four-legged furry creatures "dog" and everything that grows in the park, be it grass or bush or towering maple, "flower."

Child-language researchers have found that most children are able to discriminate visually among the people or objects that they group together this way but simply lack the vocabulary to name them separately. A parent can help by supplying the missing specific words and indicating the distinction — touching a tree while repeating "tree," for instance, and then presenting a blossom while saying "flower."

A toddler such as this one playing peekaboo learns some of the basic rules of conversation through games even before she can speak in complete sentences. Peekaboo, for instance, teaches children to take turns.

Making a common word exclusive

Some children unintentionally achieve the opposite result — reducing the effectiveness of their vocabularies — by a practice researchers call overrestriction. Just as the child imagines her own name to belong exclusively to her, so she may give a newly learned word a personal definition, relating directly to her own experience. Thus the family's collie is a "dog," without a doubt, but when the child meets the neighbor's miniature poodle, she may not know what to call the animal. As time goes on and the youngster adds more words to her speaking vocabulary — typically about 11 new words per month in this period — she modifies her understanding of the meanings of words she already knows until they more nearly match the meanings used by the adults around her.

Early pronunciations

A beginning talker has a hard time mastering adult-sounding pronunciations until she literally gets her tongue under control. Her biggest problems are in forming some consonants. Her solutions are not random but systematic, as she makes practical substitutions or deletions for the sounds she cannot summon. Thus the word "ball" becomes "baw" because *w* is the natural stand-in for the hard to form *l* at this age. The word "stop" becomes "top" and "water," "war," because the early speaker cannot manage either a consonant cluster (such as the letters *s* and *t* together) or a two-syllable word with ease. Even relatively simple one-syllable words may suffer in translation as final consonants are dropped, with words such as "bed" becoming "beh" and "hat," "ha." But since Mom and Dad are close observers and fast learners, they can usually figure out their youngster's message.

Breakthrough at 18 months

When a typical child is about a year and a half old, he reaches a kind of verbal threshold. His pronunciation is sharpening daily. With about 50 words he can claim as his own, he embarks on a powerful surge in vocabulary growth, acquiring new and more precisely applied words at a greatly accelerated rate of up to 80 per month. Some authorities think that the child's final victory over the mechanics of walking, which also often occurs at around 18 months, may account for the notable speed-up in language skill, in that the toddler is free to devote a greater share of his attention to talking.

Other specialists link this growth spurt to the youngster's realization that everything has its own name. Before this, each word he acquired existed in a kind of singular splendor, much as though the thing it described was somehow uniquely endowed with an associated sound. But somewhere around the 50-word level, the child comes to realize that there is a whole system of meaningful sounds available to him, that objects such as chair and hat, actions such as run and jump, and qualities such as hot and cold and nice have names that he can learn and use in communicating with others. And by this time, most youngsters have learned the words for several colors, although they may not always use the words correctly. Many young children seem to fall head over heels in love with talking, and they pursue new words with a passion.

Two-word sentences Around this time, the toddler begins constructing two-word sentences. These sentences are much like two-word telegrams, in that the child assembles the essentials of his message in the most economical form possible. Virtually all of the toddler's early sentences are pared down to two of the three grammatical units — subject, verb and object — that characterize the typical adult sentence.

Some of the youngster's two-word telegrams are subject-verb, as in "Baby hit." Some are verb-object: "Hit ball." And some are subject-object, as in "Baby ball." Together they indicate that the child is beginning to grasp the relationship of the doer, the action and the done-to, and thus the rudiments of the grammatically complete subject-verb-object sentence arrangement that he will make use of later.

Articles, pronouns, prepositions and auxiliary verbs, the trimmings of adult speech, are still missing from the child's sentences, as are many subtleties of meaning, but the basic intent of the message is usually pretty clear. Now your youngster has the ability to make assertions that even strangers can understand. For example, he can indicate location by saying "There cookie," or "Bubba here."

During this period he also begins to use modifiers, commenting on the quality of an object by adding words such as "pretty" and "big" and "good." He learns to express possession, as in "My milk," and "Daddy shoe." Perhaps more useful from his point of view is that the two-word telegram makes his forthright requests and refusals even clearer. No one can mistake the meaning of "More book!" or "Want toy!" or "No eat!" And he now can ask questions, using two-word sentences that are delivered with a rising inflection, as in "Mama go?" or "Sit chair?" The two-word sentence seems to be a simple way to get around the uncertainties of the more complex grammatical constructions that a child hears adults use. ∴

Two to Three Years

At about two years of age a child is likely to abandon most of her made-up words for real ones. Some of the new words express abstract concepts rather than specific names for things, which indicates that she is organizing her environment into manageable, recognizable categories. Now she may know not only the word for apple but also for fruit, and she can think about the family's pet not only as "Dog" but also as a dog and perhaps as an animal. Virtually all of the new words come from her personal experience — what she sees at home, on the street, at the playground. Nouns still outnumber other words, but she has prepositions such as "in" and "on" under partial control and is using more and more verbs, although mainly only in the present tense.

Longer telegrams

The two-year-old's sentences are still usually telegraphic, but she can now manage as many as four words in sequence, sometimes in standard subject-verb-object order. Soon she starts to produce complex sentences containing what linguists call subordinate clauses, object phrases and embedded clauses, as well as other structural elements that elaborate on the main thought.

While there is great variety in the age at which children begin using these different forms, virtually all youngsters follow the same sequence. One early type of complex sentence might be on the order of "I see you sit down," in which the object of the verb "see" is no longer the simple "you" but the whole clause "you sit down." Several other verbs that invite such constructions will probably pop into a child's speech during this stage, including "watch," "want," "look," "like," "need," "make," "ask" and "let." Other complex sentences likely to appear around the same time are those featuring clauses introduced by "how," "when" and "who," as in "I show you how to do it."

Simple sentences joined into compound sentences by the conjunctions "and" and "but" come next, an indication of the child's developing awareness that facts or events sometimes are related to one another. "Because" and "so" appear a bit later, usually toward the end of the third year, marking the youngster's discovery of cause and effect. Interestingly, two seemingly sim-

Language Milestones
- Understands but does not always correctly use common personal pronouns such as "me," "you," "mine."
- Understands and begins to use a few prepositions, such as "on," "under," "with."
- Uses three-word and four-word sentences.
- Correctly employs the present and past tenses of regular verbs.
- Adds suffix "-ing" to verbs to denote temporary action: "Dog running."
- Begins to refer to future events.
- Refers to self by name.
- Uses regular plurals (those formed by adding s to a word).
- Distinguishes objects by using demonstratives such as "this" or "that" before articles ("This a car") or adjectives ("This big car").
- Uses helping-verb structure, often getting the words wrong: "Me gonna play" for "I'm going to play."

A mother makes outlandish clown faces for her child, who tries to imitate them. In attempting to ape the funny faces, the youngster incidentally practices moving tongue, lips and jaw quickly and accurately, skills that are necessary for the enunciation of words.

ple conjunctions, "before" and "after," as in the sentence "I tie my shoes after I put on my hat," may not become part of speech for several years to come, partly because the order of words often does not correspond to the order of events.

Cadence and pronunciation

During this year the child's tonal expression and speech rhythm begin to make his sentences flow more like an adult's. His pronunciations, on the other hand, are still off the mark as much as 50 percent of the time. In fact, some words that he said correctly when he was younger may come out all wrong now. This could be because he has learned some new lesson about pronunciation and is employing it where it does not apply.

During this or the next year, your child might go through a phase in which he seems to be stuttering. In the great majority of cases it is a harmless temporary glitch, probably caused by excitement or by the fact that, for the moment, he thinks of what he wants to say faster than he can reproduce the words. Lisping is another common phenomenon for the two-year-old and may continue for several years, because the *s* sound, produced by passing the breath between the tip of the tongue and the gum ridge behind the upper teeth, is among the more difficult speech sounds to master. The less attention you pay to such difficulties the better. Correcting the child will make him self-conscious, and it may diminish his pleasure in talking with you. Instead, be a good listener, concentrating on content rather than style. And make your own conversation a model of smooth, deliberate speech so that he has a good example to follow.

Grammatical agreement

During this stage your child becomes increasingly aware that many words change form to suit circumstances. "His" becomes "her" depending upon who is being talked about, "book" becomes "books" when there is more than one, and verb endings adapt to who and how many are doing something: "He goes, I go, they go." From his observations of adult speech the child formulates a set of sensible working rules for himself. Thus he confidently forms the plurals "toys," "shoes" and "cats" and logically generalizes to produce "foots," "mans," "sheeps" and "tooths." And he can use many regular verbs in past, present and future tenses, but stumbles when he tries to do the same to irregular verbs ("I runned home."), whose forms must be learned one by one. Ironically, when his vocabulary was more limited and he was unaware of the rules, he may have said "feet" and "teeth" correctly and found the right path through the twists and turns of some irregular verbs simply by mimicking adult speech. ⋰

Three to Four Years

About the time the average child turns three, she may attempt with a little encouragement from her parents to enrich her fast-growing vocabulary with a few big words — grown-up style, many-syllable words such as "investigate" or "remarkable." About this time, too, she may learn some nursery rhymes, and she will enjoy singing along with a parent or a record.

The typical three-year-old's talk is full of questions. Where, what and why questions begin to appear first; whens do not come until later, as her sense of time becomes stronger. At this stage a sign of an improving understanding of time is more precise use of verb tenses, although she still slips up frequently. Her listening skills are also improving, and she may be able to sit attentively for as long as 20 minutes to hear a story, especially if it is a familiar one and she can share in telling what will happen next. The youngster's developing sense of humor is often revealed in her enjoyment of descriptions of improbable events or absurd combinations.

Language as a social tool

Your three-year-old may gleefully indulge in swear words and toilet talk, knowing full well that many grownups disapprove. At the same time that he is displaying this kind of rebelliousness, he probably is also learning to understand some of the underlying social messages that are expressed by the phrasing or tone of speech, rather than by the actual words spoken. He comes to know that certain remarks are not to be taken literally but have other, indirect, meanings. Take for example the parental question, "How many times do I have to tell you to stop scribbling on the wall?" The child of three and a half is likely to realize that his mother does not want a numerical answer but is issuing a command. At this age, too, he may learn to temper his own voice to reflect friendliness or anger or some other feeling, and to judge when another speaker is serious or joking, based on the manner of speech. Many children even have the verbal sensitivity now to adjust their speech to the age level of their listener, so that you may hear a youngster who is almost four slowing his speech and using simpler words when addressing a younger child.

Other advances

During this year most children develop a greater understanding of words that point out which particular object or event is being referred to — such as "this," "that" and "those" — and words that distinguish by location, such as "there" and "here." The achievement is notable, since a child must be able to juggle several items or viewpoints in his mind simultaneously in order to comprehend such distinctions. To understand "Stay there, but roll the ball here," he must hold his own position while imagining himself in the speaker's place, too.

Now, also, a child may begin to grasp passive sentences, although many children do not develop a real understanding of the passive-sentence form until later. Before this step he has had a working familiarity only with the active voice, in which the subject is mentioned first and does something to the object: "The girl kicked the boy." He might well have misunderstood a passive-voice construction, thinking that "The boy was kicked by the girl" meant the boy was doing the kicking, because the boy was mentioned first. Now, however, he may have a better chance of understanding a passive sentence correctly. Most children do not consistently use passive sentences correctly until they are seven or eight years old.

A child between three and four will sometimes correct herself in mid-sentence, an indication that she now consciously thinks about grammatical rules: "The boy runned . . . ran to the store." She also starts using what linguists call contingent queries, conversational devices for asking another speaker to clarify, explain or elaborate on a remark. An example is the following exchange between two children who are nearly four years of age. Aaron says, "I got a floaty boat for my birthday," to which Mary responds, "What kinda boat?" Aaron: "A floaty boat for when I have a bath." Mary: "Oh, I've got two of those boats." Mary's query, "What kind?" is contingent on, and gets Aaron to clarify, his opening statement.

Up until now, negative statements probably have been formed on a hit-or-miss basis, with the child sticking a "no" or "not" somewhere in a sentence, according to her best guess: "Not bed," "Eat no peas today," "No run in the house." But somewhere in the first half of this year, she acquires "can't," "won't" and "don't." And as she approaches her fourth birthday, with the help of newly learned flexibility in arranging word sequences, she makes a giant leap toward properly formed negative sentences. Thus a child nearly four may say, "I cannot eat more," and "Isn't that pretty?" In her enthusiasm, she may produce double negatives like, "I didn't eat no ice cream." You can help her out of such tangles by gently confirming but rephrasing her statement: "That's right, you didn't eat *any* ice cream." Words such as "any," "much" and "enough" — modifiers often used with negatives — are usually among the last common terms to be acquired by youngsters, probably because they represent elusive notions of quantification. ⟡

Counter-clockwise starting at upper left, a three-year-old responds to requests from a parent to place his Teddy bear "on," "under" and "beside" a chair. His actions demonstrate and reinforce his understanding of prepositions. Children understand language concepts best when they learn them through an activity.

Four Years and Older

Before starting school, your child probably will have acquired most of the grammatical skills that he will need as an adult. At four years of age he makes sentences that are still short in comparison with those of older children, averaging five to six words each, and the thoughts he expresses are relatively unsophisticated. But he understands the social and private power of language, has the underlying principles of syntax in place and can produce well-constructed sentences of increasing variety in which the plurals, pronouns and even verb tenses are correct more often than not. By six years of age, with about 2,600 words on call for use and perhaps another 9,000 or so that he understands, he is by any reasonable measure an effective communicator.

A need to talk

Speech tends to be a necessary accompaniment to just about every activity in the four-year-old's day. When she is not conversing with a parent or caregiver, she may be ordering herself about, chatting with a real or imaginary playmate, or singing to herself. Typically she is a colorful storyteller, especially of tall tales. Because her memory skills as well as her sense of time are improving, she may start spinning long, fantastical stories that feature a recognizable "Once upon a time" beginning, a middle and an end. Sometimes she accompanies her descriptions with dramatic acting. Characters may be difficult for parents to keep straight and the action may be hard to follow, but the young narrator clearly knows what is happening and wants very much to get her story across without interruption. Often the plot revolves around violent death and other calamitous events, but parents should not be overly concerned. For youngsters this age, imagined mayhem is a normal device for dealing with the natural anxieties of life.

Your four- or five-year-old's enthusiasm for communication, coupled with her natural candor and lack of social inhibitions, can occasionally lead to embarrassing revelations outside the home. She is likely to discuss family secrets with anyone who cares to listen. Since the youngster cannot be expected to understand what is considered a private matter and what is all right for public consumption, the most reliable way to curb your child's gossipy ways is to exercise some discretion in what you do and say in front of her.

So-called dirty words, scatology, boasting, bragging and exaggerations worthy of Paul Bunyan are also to be expected of youngsters at this stage. If such talk does not suit your family standards of behavior, you may wish to try to curb the use of these expressions through calm discussion about how inappro-

Language Milestones

- Understands and begins to use opposites such as "big" and "small," and "high" and "low."
- Describes recent experiences in the order in which they occurred.
- Follows complex, three-step directions in the right sequence.
- Rhymes words.
- Consistently uses past tenses of irregular verbs — such as "went," "drank," "ate" — correctly.
- Uses some irregular plurals — "mice," "sheep" — properly.
- Uses articles "a" and "the" consistently.
- Uses possessive form of nouns correctly.
- Answers the telephone and gets the person requested by the caller.
- Defines a word: "A knife is something sharp that you use to cut things."
- Responds appropriately to questions about quantity ("How much . . .?"), duration ("How long . . .?"), distance ("How far . . .?") and timing ("When . . .?").

priate they are. But from the standpoint of language development, they are just another natural way to practice verbal skills.

Pronunciation

The preschooler is likely to have continuing difficulty sounding some consonants and combinations of consonants. The most common problems are with sounds known as fricatives, such as *sh, th, f, z* and *s.* In some instances a child may be able to produce a problem sound when she is not trying, as in the case of the youngster who says "fick" when she wants "thick" but says "thick" when she means "sick." Only 50 percent of children will have mastered all the sounds needed to speak the language by the age of five, and as late as seven, 10 percent will still have difficulty with at least one sound.

The emerging poet

Children enjoy playing with language and ideas. This becomes particularly evident at about the age of four, although even younger children can turn memorable phrases now and then. Between four and five years of age, many youngsters begin to see the world as a more intriguingly complex place than they realized before. They want to talk about new feelings, sights, qualities and experiences that their limited vocabularies have no words to describe. So they may use words they already know in new ways, solving the problem of conveying difficult-to-express ideas while at the same time giving rein to their poetic spirits. The metaphors that result can be positively delightful to jaded adult ears. Thus a four-year old whose fingers brush a nettle growing in the fields can report that he has been "bitten by a bumblebee plant," the youngster shivering from the cold can say that his "teeth are typing," and the child who sees a bald man can describe him as having "a barefoot head."

Parents should not presume from this that their child is destined to be a poet. Children of this age are interested in imitating adults, including saying things the way adults say them. Trying to perform like the adults they know, most youngsters will abandon such lyrical observation and highly creative use of language in favor of more conventional expression. The onset of this conventional phase, which corresponds roughly to the beginning of formal schooling, need not signal the end of a child's creativity with words, however. Encouragement of a lot of reading and writing throughout the school years can foster continued language flexibility and experimentation. ⁖

Relying on an increasing memory span as well as her picture book to remind her of the details, a preschooler recounts a story to her father. Although few of them could express the notion, four-year-olds such as this one are aware of the importance of language as a tool for learning, communicating and creating, and they know how books work.

Common Speech Problems

Although you should not be unduly concerned if your child's progress in various areas of speech and language development lags somewhat behind the average timetable described on the preceding pages, neither should you ignore signs of a serious problem. About 5 percent of children experience developmental deviations or delays of a magnitude that indicates those youngsters may need professional help. They may have physical, neurological or emotional problems that interfere with their ability to understand language or to speak. The first five years of life are critical in the treatment of such problems. So if your child displays any of the warning signs described in the box opposite, consult your pediatrician, who may refer you to a speech-language pathologist or an audiologist — a hearing specialist.

Pronunciation

Among the most common speech disorders that can afflict a child is an inability to pronounce or articulate some words or letter-combinations long after his peers have mastered them. The cause may be a hearing problem, perhaps congenital, perhaps resulting from repeated infections of the middle ear in early childhood. Even when hearing loss is mild, a child may not be able to distinguish and therefore cannot articulate certain consonants. He may also have trouble capturing conventional voice rhythms and intonations, which are picked up chiefly through imitating others. Prompt attention to the hearing problem, together with speech therapy, usually can bring the child up to age-performance levels, after which he should progress normally. More severe hearing loss requires more extensive remedies.

Stuttering

All children from about two to six years old are occasionally disfluent — that is, their speech is sometimes interrupted by unintended midsentence pauses or repeated words or sounds. This kind of normal disfluency, the result of a young mind groping for vocabulary or new pronunciations or better sentence construction, may involve repeating whole words or phrases ("I want . . . I want to go home."), changing a sentence in midstream ("Can we go . . . I want to go home."), filling pauses with "ahhhs" and "ummms," and long empty pauses.

But when the problem is frequent repetition of a consonant or part of a word ("b-b-b-ball"), it may not be normal disfluency but instead a case of stuttering — chronic, involuntary spasms of the speech muscles that cause interruptions of speech or prolongations of sounds. Another indication of stuttering, or stammering, is a sound held for longer than a second while the child tries to get it out ("the b---all"). More boys stutter than girls. The cause of stuttering is not known for sure, but heredity seems to be a factor. Almost 70 percent of stutterers come from families with at least one other stutterer. And the condition is closely associated with stress and fear. Children who stutter often show tension through a trembling voice or tightened neck and face muscles, and a stutterer's stammer will worsen as stress increases.

Obviously, a parent or other adult should try to show no anxiety when listening to a stuttering child: This could worsen the child's problem. Nor is it wise to tell the child to slow down, to take a deep breath or to start over. Those suggestions can increase the stress the youngster feels. Instead, try to slow your own pace of speaking, stretching sounds and spaces between words to serve as a model for the child. Make your sentences as simple as possible so the child will not feel the need to answer in complex sentences. When possible, avoid direct questions, which pressure a child. And do not criticize his speech. However, if a child of three or older demonstrates symptoms of stuttering that last longer than eight months, do not pretend to ignore the problem. Stay calm but explain that some help may be needed and consult your child's doctor. Pretending it does not matter may tell the child that the way he talks is unimportant.

Developmental delay and other problems

Some 2 to 3 percent of three-year-old children in the U.S., two thirds of them boys, are slow to learn to speak and are diagnosed as suffering from the syndrome known as delayed language. The apparent causes range from mild brain damage to the stress of a bilingual environment to antagonisms in the family. Some delayed children will never attain adult levels of speech or other skills, but others, with the proper therapy, eventually reach or surpass a normal level. Other defects that hurt speech, such as cleft palate, malformation of the vocal cords, cerebral palsy and brain disorders, are special cases that require surgery and other special treatment. ❖

4 Learning Responsibility

With continued growth and the further development of her language and motor skills, your toddler will begin to assume responsibility for her own care and well-being. As she reaches out to master the world around her, she will need guidance and encouragement as well as day-to-day care — even though at times her insistence on doing things herself may temporarily stand in the way.

How much your child will be able to do for herself depends largely on her level of physical dexterity and motor coordination. A one-year-old cannot be expected to use a spoon without making a mess, for example, while a four-year-old will wield both spoon and fork with proficiency but still be all thumbs when it comes to handling a knife. Dressing, too, is difficult at first for young children; buttons, zippers and shoelaces may confound even the nimblest of little fingers throughout the preschool years. With increased manual dexterity, however, your child's attempts to dress herself will become more successful. She will be working on other self-help skills, too: learning how to wash her hands and brush her teeth, how to comb and shampoo her hair, and how to navigate around a host of hazards both in and outside the home. Soon the cries of "Mommy, I did it all by myself!" will become more and more frequent.

But as important as such skills are, they are mere stumbling blocks on the road to self-reliance when measured against the high hurdle of toilet training. In the past, the toddler's potty chair was too often the setting for a battle of wills between the adult eager to enforce parental authority and the child who saw each step in the toilet-training process as yet another opportunity to flex her blossoming independence. But as the following pages show, by approaching toilet training with patience and understanding — not to mention a healthy supply of humor — you can make this potentially combative process a simple and emotionally rewarding experience for both yourself and your child.

Toilet Training

For many parents and their children, toilet training is an easy and relatively uneventful rite of passage. But for others, the bathroom becomes the unlikely scene of a power struggle, as the determined child meets an equally determined parent in an all-out clash of wills.

This emotional tug-of-war can be easily avoided in many instances merely by waiting until the child is ready — physically, mentally and emotionally — to take on the responsibility for toileting by himself. Heralded by certain unmistakable signs of readiness *(box, right),* that moment usually arrives sometime after the child is 18 months old, the age when a toddler's maturing nervous system completes the link between brain and bowel and bladder. Only then is he physically capable of controlling his excretory functions, and only then can he begin to understand exactly what it is his mother or father wants him to do — and what all the fuss is about when he does not do it.

The question of timing

Shortly after his first birthday, your child may display signs of this increased physical maturity: showing some regularity in his bowel habits, for instance. You may also notice other, less obvious signs of readiness prompted by your youngster's developing mental and emotional maturity. By the age of two, he may enjoy putting things in containers and show some understanding that toys, clothes and even bowel movements have their proper places. Your child may also show an increased willingness to tackle new skills — and obvious pride at success — as well as a greater tendency to imitate you and your spouse. Together these

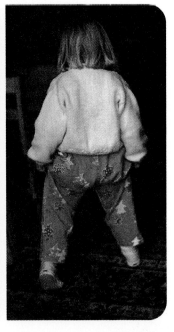

Is Your Child Ready to Begin?

A child who is ready for daytime control may:
- have regular bowel movements.
- pause, grunt or change facial expressions while he is having a bowel movement.
- announce that a bowel movement is imminent or has just passed.
- look around for a private place in which to crouch while he is having a bowel movement — even when he is wearing a diaper.

- stay dry for one or two hours during the day or wake up dry from naps.
- complain when his diaper becomes wet or soiled.
- show greater self-awareness about bodily functions and his role in controlling them.
- want to be clean and tidy.
- request to have his diaper removed in order to use the potty or indicate that he wants to start wearing underwear instead of diapers.

A child who is ready for nighttime control may:
- have fewer daytime accidents.
- be upset by accidents.
- stay dry for three or four hours during the day.
- wake up dry from naps or in the morning after a night's sleep.
- get up at night in order to urinate in the toilet.
- ask if he can stop wearing diapers when he goes to bed at night.

signs point the way toward true readiness for toilet training.

By postponing toilet training until your child is both physically and psychologically ready, you may decrease the overall length of time it takes to achieve control. Recent research shows that regardless of when children begin their training, they achieve daytime bowel and bladder control at an average age of 28 months. In other words, whether you start toileting your child at 11 months or at 26 months, chances are he will not be fully trained until about 28 months. Nighttime control follows, with most children staying dry through the night by three to four and a half years of age, although some entirely normal children will continue to wet the bed for many months longer and have occasional accidents throughout the preschool years.

Starting too early Current research on toilet training flies in the face of earlier attitudes and practices, which dictated that a child should be planted on the potty before he was barely able to walk, and worse, made to sit there until he performed to the parent's satisfaction. Even today, well-meaning relatives and friends may try to pressure you into giving your child an early start on toilet training. But by giving in to that pressure, you only set the stage for what will ultimately be a long and often frustrating learning process, one marked by anger, resentment and mutual distrust that may persist long after the diaper days are behind you.

It is unfortunate that in their eagerness to prod their youngsters down the path to self-sufficiency, parents sometimes forget that babies want to be babied. The pressure to make the child more independent may in fact force him to cling tighter to babyhood. Moreover, when these early efforts to toilet train the child fail, as they almost always do, the parents only increase the likelihood of resistance to later training.

Some experts suggest that early toileting can result in negative associations with the toilet itself. The child may not comprehend his parents' obsession with the potty and perhaps their subsequent anger at his failure to satisfy their expectations. The struggles over toilet training can become a negative factor in the development of the child's self-image.

Preparation for training

As your toddler nears her second birthday and shows some signs of readiness, you can begin the process of toilet training. It is best to divide the training process itself into two parts: a preparation phase, during which the child has the chance to grow used to the idea of toileting, followed by a more active learning phase.

During the preparation phase — which can be as brief as a week or as long as several months, depending on your child's progress — your goal is simply to help her understand how her body works and to show her what the toilet is and what it is used for. You should not expect her to use the potty regularly at this point or to exercise bowel or bladder control with any consistency. Nor should you trade in her diapers for underpants. All of those things can wait until the learning phase.

At the outset of training, let your child sit on the potty whenever she wishes, with or without her clothes on, just to get used to the idea. During these relaxed visits to the bathroom, the company of a favorite stuffed animal will be more reassuring than that of an anxious parent.

The importance of communication

For training to be effective, your child must understand what you are saying and must be able to tell you when she needs to use the potty. During the preparation phase, and probably earlier, you will want to teach her some simple words to describe her bowel and bladder functions. Such expressions as "bm" and "tinkle" — or any others you are comfortable with — are easiest for the little one to remember and repeat. Using these words, you can then help her to associate the sensations of excretion with the results in her diaper by taking advantage of those times when you notice her having a bowel movement to point out, for example, that she is "making a bm."

Diaper-changing sessions also provide ideal opportunities to slip in some casual words of encouragement, perhaps by mentioning that "When you start using the potty, you'll be able to wear big-girl pants instead of diapers," or by capitalizing on your child's developing desire for cleanliness by pointing out how good it feels to be clean and dry after changing the soiled diaper.

And finally, since two-year-olds have a natural desire to imitate their elders, another good way for your toddler to discover what the toilet is used for is by observing others. You can demonstrate or explain to your child that big people like Mommy and Daddy use the toilet and that she will, too, when she is bigger. She should also have ample opportunities to observe other children using the toilet, either siblings or friends.

Your child's first potty

The preparation period is also the time to buy or borrow a potty and introduce it into the home. There are several kinds of potties available, such as inserts that slip over the seat of the regular toilet and freestanding, child-size toilets. If you opt for the insert you will also need to provide the child with a stepping stool; little boys will need the stool later on as well to stand on while urinating. However, most parents and child-care experts agree that the freestanding potty makes the best choice, for unlike a seat insert it offers the child a measure of security, both in having her feet on the floor and in reducing any fear the child might have of falling into the big toilet.

Introducing the potty

If you are using a freestanding potty, place it on the bathroom floor next to the toilet and encourage your toddler to sit on the potty if she wants to, perhaps while you sit on the adult toilet beside her. There is no need at this point to remove her clothing or to urge her actually to use the potty. Instead, let her explore the potty at will to get comfortable with it.

After the child has had a week or so to get used to her new possession, ask her if she would like to sit on the potty without her diaper on. Try after breakfast, if that is her accustomed time for a bowel movement. If she agrees and manages to urinate or defecate in the potty, by all means express your delight and praise her. Do not overdo it, however, since too much praise can instill a fear of failure in the toddler. When she is ready to get up, let her do so immediately. Under no circumstances should you restrain the child on the potty or scold her for lack of success.

As with any other skill, practice makes perfect, so once your youngster seems to understand what is expected of her on the potty, you can try to establish a daily routine. Once a day — after a meal, perhaps, if that is the best time, or else when you notice she is about to have a bowel movement — take the child to the bathroom and suggest that she try to use the potty. Let her sit there for five or 10 minutes at most — or for a shorter period if she chooses to get up. Praise her if praise is due or else reassure her that another time she may be more successful.

Remember, this is still the preparation period; you should not expect or demand that your child perform on cue. If the child does settle into a daily routine and merrily trots off to the toilet as the need arises, count yourself lucky. On the other hand, if the youngster resists — even after a short period of success — back off and wait a few days or a week before trying again. Remember, the key to success is to relax and let your child set the pace.

Beginning the learning phase

At some point during the preparation phase of toilet training, it is likely that your child will start asking to have his diaper removed in order to go to the potty or will express a desire to wear underpants like his older friends or siblings. If so, this is your cue to shift from the preparation phase to the learning phase.

You should begin by setting a date to buy underpants. Of course, the switch to underpants does not mean that there will not be accidents — perhaps plenty of them. And it does not mean that your toddler will not have to wear a diaper at night and during naps for a while longer. But it does let him know that he is a big boy now and should use the potty as big boys do.

In choosing a day for the change to underpants, be careful to avoid any periods of potential stress in the youngster's life. Do not, for example, launch the learning phase of toilet training following the birth of a new baby or in the wake of some family illness or a change in baby-sitters. The added excitement of the switch to underpants and the pressure to stay clean and dry will only make matters worse.

On the day set for this important shopping trip, by all means let your child accompany you to the store and help select his new underwear. Buy at least a dozen, in order to be prepared for the inevitable accidents. When you slip his first pair onto him, remind him that he is a big boy and will have to use the potty.

The Trials of Earlier Generations

In startling contrast to the relaxed rite of passage espoused by child-care experts today, toilet training in the past was all too often a gauntlet of harsh and sometimes bizarre procedures.

As recently as the 1930s, in a book entitled *Growing Superior Children,* a respected pediatrician advised mothers of newborns to practice "maternal diligence" that would be rewarded with proper bowel control by the time their babies were three months old. Even more incredibly, bladder training, the author noted, would follow in a week or two. During the same period, a noted behavioral psychologist was suggesting that a baby, starting at the age of eight months, was to be strapped into a special toilet seat and left alone in the bathroom — the better to discourage "dawdling, loud conversation and generally unsocial and delinquent behavior" — until

he had done his duty.

It is little wonder, then, that today many grandparents maintain proudly that their children were trained by 12 months or earlier — despite the fact that it is physiologically impossible for a child that young to control his bowel or bladder. In truth it was the adults who were trained: Having learned to recognize the signs of an imminent bowel movement, they became adept at whisking the infant to the bathroom and making lucky catches in the potty as the baby passively reacted to nature's call.

A century earlier, parents and nannies were being trained in a similar fashion. Child-rearing experts of the 1830s advised a mother to hold her two-month-old infant in a sitting position on the chamber pot before, during and after each meal so the baby would be "clean" by the age of four months.

Nor was the 19th-century bed-wetter overlooked. One advisor of the mid-1800s recommended that the child be made to sleep on straw and be rubbed frequently with a stiff brush. Another advice-giver of that age advocated a somewhat more enlightened approach, suggesting cold-water baths before bed and touting "the useful invention, Macintosh sheeting" — a waterproof material used in raincoats.

And what could the child of the 1800s hope to gain from early toilet training and remedial therapy? He would, wrote one proponent of early toileting, become "a comfort to all around, and a great saver of dresses and furniture." While words such as these may have reassured many parents of the day, a century later child-care manuals were blaming subsequent psychological difficulties on the very same toileting practices.

Encourage him to tell Mommy or Daddy when he needs to go. If you want, you can take him to the potty now, just once, and suggest that he urinate. Praise him if he does. A little while later, take a moment to remind him again that he is not wearing a diaper and should let you know if he needs to potty.

When accidents occur

Accidents are bound to happen, and no doubt the child will be more than a little upset by the fact that he has soiled or wet his new pants — but you should not be. Resist the tendency to scold or punish. Do not even disapprove; after all, it is an accident. Instead, reassure him that "Next time you may be able to tell Mommy or Daddy you have to tinkle," then calmly lead him to the bathroom and encourage him to sit on the potty "just in case there's any more that has to come out" before finally cleaning him up. Throughout the day, remind him that he should go to the potty if he needs to. But do not be too insistent.

And when will the accidents end? The best answer — in time — is unfortunately the vaguest, and it may be small comfort to the parent who seems to be spending all her time changing pants and mopping up puddles. Eventually, however, the number of accidents does taper off, although it is not unusual for three- and four-year-olds occasionally to wet their pants. This is nothing to be worried about; complete daytime bladder control almost always comes by the time the child starts kindergarten.

Looking at picture books about toilet training — and identifying with the people who are his fictional counterparts — can help a youngster put his training experiences in perspective. Here, a mother shows her son a book demonstrating that his adult heroes — "even firemen" — use the toilet.

Teaching proper hygiene

Proper hygiene is an important part of toilet training and is another lesson you will have to teach your child as he begins to take on the responsibility of going to the toilet by himself. Handwashing is simple enough and can even be fun, especially if you equip the bathroom with liquid soap in a pump bottle, which most children find a great treat. Flushing, too, is a source of amusement to many children. Wiping, however, can be a chore.

It is best not to trouble the child about wiping at first: Most parents expect to have to wipe their children throughout the initial preparation period and the early days of the learning phase. Eventually, however, you will want your child to learn to wipe himself and, in fact, in his eagerness to be a big boy, he may very well jump at the chance. But some children may not be so

Training Tales

66 Alan always competed with his older brother for our attention. When we started training him he figured out real fast that sitting on the toilet was a sure way to get it. He would cry wolf, then chat or sing songs on the potty while we sat there waiting for him to finish. When we realized what was going on, we started leaving him, checking back every few minutes. We saved the heavy-duty attention for other times. 99

66 Toilet training seemed impossible until a friend of mine suggested making a game out of it — and so we invented 'sink the ship.' I put a toilet tissue or a small piece of paper into the toilet and had Tony try to sink the paper with a steady stream of urine. It was a good idea because it motivated him to try until he had control of the process. 99

66 Once we left our three-month-old in his portable chair for just a moment in the living room and returned to find him gone. We raced around frantically looking for him and found that Harris, our newly-trained three-year-old, had dragged his little brother to the bathroom to keep him company while he sat on the potty. Harris said that he wanted to teach the baby the correct way to go to the bathroom. 99

66 Marcy enjoyed making a special routine out of trips to the potty. I would count each step with her as we climbed the stairs to the bathroom. Once she was on the toilet, I would tell her to listen to the sound the 'tinkle' made hitting the water. She was pleased each time she made the 'tinkle noise.' If she had to wait awhile, I tried to take her mind off the problem by reading or singing to her. 99

66 Benjy, at three, was slow in his toilet training, and maybe we worried too much. One night we were having a dinner party. To make it all go smoothly, I hired a sitter so I wouldn't have to put the kids to bed myself. Just as I was ushering our guests into the dining room, Benjy burst in with his pants still down. He shouted: 'Momma! Momma! Three big pieces.' I just wanted to die. 99

66 We left our two-year-old with my mother for two weeks when we had to travel, and we returned to find Arlene potty-trained. But two months later, she began having accidents. It turned into a power struggle, with Arlene refusing to go to the bathroom and then five minutes later wetting her pants. Against my mother's advice, I put Arlene back into diapers. I sensed that she had been under a lot of pressure. She asked me if it was all right to tinkle in her diaper, and I assured her it was okay. Now, six weeks later, she takes off her diaper for a bowel movement but not for a tinkle. I'm in no rush: She'll come back to it when she's ready. Of course, I'm not telling my mother about it. 99

keen about embracing independence and may want their parents to continue to do the wiping for them. One solution to this problem is to teach your child to wipe and then offer to come in and check on how he is doing. In time, he will be fending for himself and you can dispense with the need to check on his progress. When teaching a little girl to wipe, be sure to instruct her to wipe in a backward direction, from front to rear, to avoid spreading germ-bearing fecal matter to tender vaginal tissues and to reduce the chance of urinary-tract infections.

Nighttime control For most children, daytime control precedes nighttime control by several months. That being the case, your toddler-in-training will have to rely on a diaper for naps and nights. She may resist, since understandably she will not be too eager to relinquish her newly acquired big-girl pants. Simply explain to her that all small children wear a diaper to bed and that when she gets a little bigger she will not need diapers anymore. Reassure her that she can put her underpants back on as soon as she gets up.

One of the earliest signs of readiness for nighttime control is an obvious decline in the number of daytime accidents. The child may also wake up dry on some mornings or occasionally after a nap, or she may go three to four hours during the day without urinating, a sure sign that her bladder is maturing. Quite often a toddler may ask to forgo a diaper at night.

Once a child is ready, you can begin nighttime training merely by removing the diaper to see if she stays dry through the night. Accidents are to be expected and should your child wake up crying, your response should be the same as for any toileting accident: Resist scolding and instead reassure her that "These things happen," and "Maybe tomorrow night you'll stay dry." Then change the bed with minimal fuss. If necessary, you can plug in a night light and place the potty in the child's bedroom at night to encourage her to get up to urinate if she needs to.

By the time they are three years old, many children are staying dry through the night. However, others may not achieve night-time control until they are four years of age and sometimes older, a situation that can result in understandable worry for the parent and increased anxiety for the child. And yet, since control depends on bladder capacity and neuromuscular maturity, which develop at the child's own individual pace, there is actually no need for concern in most cases.

If your child seems to be making little progress in mastering this new skill and is continually wetting the bed night after night, you may have misjudged her readiness and it is probably wise to return to diapers for a time. Be sure to reassure her that there is nothing to be ashamed about and that as soon as she gets a little bigger she can dispense with diapers for good.

Looking ahead "You think it's going to go on forever," said one mother when asked to recall her toilet-training experiences with her son, "then all of a sudden it's over." Indeed, it is often difficult for parents to keep things in perspective during the weeks or months they spend ushering their children through the toilet-training process. But in the end, all your patience and persistence will pay off in the pride and confidence instilled in your newly trained child — who has, after all, just mastered her first major lesson in social responsibility. ❖

Common Toileting Concerns

No matter how cooperative a child is, and no matter how patient the parent, toilet training may be difficult. Some children, for example, may suffer normal lapses of control for a day or two or even a week. Others experience problems in developing consistent nighttime control, even after weeks or months of trying. And a few otherwise healthy, happy two- and three-year-olds will display no interest in toilet training, until you begin to wonder, as one mother of a three-year-old did, whether "my child is going to be the oldest living human in diapers." You can rest assured that many of the so-called problems are not really problems at all but normal setbacks on the developmental path. Only rarely is there any need for professional help, since in most instances the best cure is simply to watch and wait.

When your child is not interested

The chances are that by the time your child is two to two and a half years old, he will be showing some or all of the signs of readiness for bowel and bladder training. But suppose your toddler seems to understand his bodily functions, is staying dry for a few hours at a time, tells you when he has had a bowel movement, even has his own potty and knows what it is there for — and yet week after week he contentedly goes through the day wetting and soiling his diapers. Even worse, he seems completely uninterested in using the potty. What should you do?

For some parents, the answer is simple: Do nothing but wait until the child shows interest, as he surely will in due course. But other parents choose to take the initiative themselves, suggesting a switch to underpants and proceeding from there into the learning phase *(page 114)*. As long as the child is old enough — at least 28 months for a girl and six months older for a boy — and cooperative, such a solution is entirely within bounds. You should, of course, make sure that the switch to underpants does not coincide with any other change in the youngster's lifestyle — a new baby, for example, or a move to a new house — and make every effort to avoid putting undue pressure on the child.

Dealing with resistance

There is nothing unusual about a child who resists your efforts to toilet train him. Very often such resistance is merely the two-year-old's way of asserting his growing independence. Resistance can also result from too early or too vigorous toilet training. And even a child who had been cooperative earlier in the training process may suddenly become obstinate and refuse to go to the potty. Some particularly stubborn children may go so far as to constipate themselves, while others may agree to sit on the potty, unproductively as it turns out, only to soil their dia-

Avoid many toileting problems by dressing your toddler in easy-to-manage clothes. Stretch pants with elasticized waistbands that she can pull up and down without assistance are ideal.

pers as soon as they get up. Here, as always where toileting is concerned, punishment and scolding have no place. Faced with resistance, your best recourse is to ignore the child's uncooperative behavior, ease up on any pressure and simply wait it out. Nearly always, within a few weeks the situation will have returned to normal. Occasionally, however, resistance may be the first indication of a toddler's secret fear of the toilet. Even more rarely, a child's resistance may have its roots in a physical problem, such as an intestinal disorder that is causing abnormally painful bowel movements. If you suspect your child is ill, seek your doctor's advice promptly.

Weathering regressions

A regression is a temporary lapse of control, and like resistance, it frequently occurs during toilet training. To the parent, the regression itself is easy enough to recognize, when after weeks or months of consistent control a child suddenly starts having accidents. Not so obvious, however, is the cause.

In the absence of any illness, regression is most likely a manifestation of stress; in dealing with it, examine your home life closely for sources of tension. Perhaps you have just brought home a new baby or returned to work after a long period at home, or maybe the child recently started nursery school. Such changes can be emotionally upsetting to the youngster, enough so that he forgets everything he once knew about toileting. On rare occasions, children use accidents more or less deliberately as a means of getting their parents' attention or as a way to register an objection to some real or imagined offense.

Happily, most periods of regression are short — often lasting less than a week — and are easily weathered with patience and understanding. Try to isolate the cause of stress and take steps to ease the pressure; often all the child needs is extra attention. Reassure him, then wait. If, despite your reassurance and patience, the toilet accidents persist, seek your doctor's advice.

Problems with nighttime control

As your child learns to master bowel and bladder control, you should not be alarmed by the occasional wet bed or a short period of nighttime regression. Simply reassure the child that all is well and clean up the mess without comment. In most instances, the regression should resolve itself within a week or so.

Occasionally, however, nighttime regressions continue for weeks or months on end; if so, it is advisable to go back to a nighttime diaper. In such cases, it is comforting to know that bed-wetting in young children is usually the result of bladder immaturity or a temporary stressful situation, not deeper psychological distress, and that nearly all children outgrow bed-wetting by the time they are ready to enter elementary school.

Toileting fears

For some children, resistance is the first indication that the toddler is frightened of the toilet. A child, for example, may develop a fear of falling into the toilet and being sucked down the drain, especially if the she has ever lost her balance and slipped through the opening in the toilet seat. A seat insert should help to allay the little one's fear, or you might suggest that she use the little potty instead of the grown-up one for a while longer.

Most toileting fears, however, center on flushing. Although many children find flushing fun — as any parent who has had to call in a plumber to dislodge a toy from the toilet drain can confirm — other youngsters see the big toilet as some monstrous and mysterious machine that roars without warning and gobbles up anything placed in its "mouth." It is understandable, then, that a child may feel that the same fate awaits her should she be so careless as to linger too long on the potty.

If your child seems frightened when you flush the toilet, simply avoid flushing while she is in the room. Wait until the child has left the bathroom and is again absorbed in play before returning to the room to empty the potty bowl and flush the toilet. You might also try putting the child in charge of removing the potty chamber and emptying it into the toilet, a task that may appeal to her sense of control. If she is old enough to understand, explain to her that she is just too big to be flushed. An even better idea is to encourage your child to do her own flushing right from the start by making it the final step in the toileting process.

Fascination with stools

Adults understand that whatever goes into a toilet should stay there and then be flushed away, but to a child a bowel movement can be a wondrous and magical thing. This notion can lead to such a fascination with the stools that the child is even tempted to touch them. While this may be disturbing to you, it is important to remember that your eagerness to flush her creation away is just as disturbing to her.

As with other toileting problems, your best response is no response. Do not lambaste the youngster with warnings that her stools are dirty. Remain calm and encourage her to look at her stools all she wants but not to touch what is in the potty.

Traveling with your trainee

This scenario is one that virtually every parent will experience sooner or later: The family is all packed for a trip and on the way to the car your youngster assures you that she does not have to go to the bathroom. Half an hour later you are racing up the next exit on the interstate, desperately hoping the service station has an available rest room.

Since any parental prompting inevitably results in an emphatic "No!" you might try making it a rule that everyone, including yourself, use the bathroom before leaving for any trip. And you can counter any potential resistance by assuring the child that she does not have to do anything on the potty if she does not need to: All you are asking is that she sit on the toilet and try.

Late bloomers Every child is different, and every child develops at her own pace. Even within families, one child may be completely toilet trained by the time she is three years old, while another may still be wetting the bed at the age of five. Nor is there anything unusual about that. In fact, studies have shown that 25 percent of all four- and five-year-olds still occasionally have accidents at night. These late bloomers will almost always outgrow this tendency, and there is no need for concern as long as your child achieves daytime control by three to four and a half years of age and nighttime control by the age of five for girls or six for boys.

Nonetheless, your late bloomer will require even more reassurance and support from you if she is to maintain her self-esteem throughout this trying period. Remind her that some other children also have accidents and wet their beds, and eventually they overcome the problem. Most important, tell her you love her no matter what. Some parents are tempted to use a mechanical bell-and-pad device, which wakes a youngster as she wets. Studies have shown, however, that this method is most appropriate for children over the age of eight, and that it is most successful when used in cooperation with a pediatrician or child psychologist.

When to seek professional help Very few children experience such long-term toileting problems that they require the help of a professional therapist. However, if by the age of five, your late bloomer seems determined not to bloom — and there seems to be no reason for the problem, such as illness or obvious stress — by all means consult your family doctor or pediatrician. Likewise, if your previously trained preschooler suddenly starts wetting or soiling her pants and you can discern no reason for the regression, you should seek professional advice — if only to rule out the possibility that there is some underlying physical cause. With the right help and with continued support and guidance from her parents, the child will in all likelihood soon be back on track. ⋰⋱

Cleanliness and Grooming

Personal hygiene seems too forbidding a label for such an easy and natural part of growing up. All by herself, your youngster will want to feel comfortable and look good, and she will glow with pride and happiness when you tell her how nice she looks. Learning how to bathe is only one of a number of grooming skills that you will help her acquire as she takes on more responsibility for her own care and well-being. In fact, long before your little one is ready for that first solo scrub in the tub, she will probably be washing her own hands and face more or less efficiently, brushing her own teeth and perhaps even combing her own hair.

In all of this, of course, you should be careful not to push too hard or too soon. The key to success is not to force these tasks on your child or turn them into unpleasant chores. As always, you should approach each item with enthusiasm tempered by patience. Remember, she is laying the groundwork for a lifetime of good grooming habits, and it is best to let her proceed at her own comfortable pace.

Frequency of bathing Though it does your heart good to see your youngster all clean and combed, children rarely stay that way for very long, and the daily accumulation of grime can be impressive. A bath every evening would certainly be in order for a highly active child who often plays outdoors. But some parents may find it unnecessary and inconvenient to bathe their children nightly, and many children would just as soon skip a daily scrub and make do with a wash-up instead.

You should feel free to adjust your youngster's bath routine to suit his needs and your schedule. The important thing is for him to bathe regularly and well. For toddlers, baths can be held to once or twice a week, with frequent diaper changes to keep their bottoms clean and occasional trips to the sink for hands and faces. As your child grows older and play becomes more vigorous, you will most likely want to increase the frequency of the baths. But by then, he will be accepting more of the responsibility for keeping himself clean, and your role will gradually become supervisory, checking to see that he has done the job adequately. Hot weather may also prompt the need for more baths, since the combination of summer temperatures and dirt-clogged pores can lead to cases of prickly heat or other skin inflammations.

Hand-puppet washcloths are fun and will encourage your youngster to wash herself. You can buy such puppets or create your own by sewing together two washcloths in a mitten-shaped pattern and decorating them with yarn.

Making bathtime fun   For most children, baths are fun: The warm, soothing water, the splashing and the sense of buoyancy can be so pleasurable that they may not want to leave the tub. Other youngsters are not such eager bathers, and it takes a little tact and imagination to coax them into the bath.

For starters, do not ever force your little one to take a bath, since interrupting his play and marching him off virtually guarantees a negative reaction. Instead, tell him in a pleasant voice that it is almost bathtime, then allow him to continue playing for a while longer. When it is time for the tub, encourage him to bring along some of his favorite toys — as long as they are waterproof and larger than the drain. Gather up a few items from the kitchen if you like; plastic cups and spoons make great bathtub toys. Adding bubble bath to the water will enhance the fun, but be sure to use a brand specially formulated to avoid irritating children's tender skin. Once your youngster is in the tub, your best bet is to get the practical part of the bath over with by washing and rinsing him quickly. Then give him ample time to play and help him invent bathtime games or songs to make it more interesting. As he grows older, he will have no trouble thinking up his own bathtub activities: washing his trucks, playing motorboat or perhaps storm at sea. And remember, no matter how mature your preschooler is, if he is younger than five you should never leave him alone in the tub.

Steps toward self-bathing   You need not wait until your child is three or four years old before teaching her how to bathe herself, since waiting will only prolong her feeling of dependence on you. As ineffective as a toddler's first efforts might be, they are a lot better than no effort at all. Begin simply by letting her play with the soap and washcloth. Later on you can teach her how to lather and rinse herself, perhaps by making a game out of washing different parts of the body until she is completely clean. For a long while yet, you will still have to intervene to make sure that she gets as clean as you like. But as time goes on, she will become more and more expert, and by the age of five, she may be capable of doing nearly the whole job herself, including shampooing her hair.

Fears of the bath   For some children, bathtime can be frightening. Often the fear can be traced to a particular cause — a fall on a slippery surface, perhaps, or an accidental encounter with too-hot water. And many a two-year-old with an immature grasp of size relationships panics at the thought that if water and bubbles and dirt go down the drain, so might he.

Whatever the reason, be patient. Bathtub fears are not unusual among toddlers, and it may take some time to overcome them. While such fears may seem unreasonable to an adult, they are only too real to your youngster, and he will need all the reassurance and understanding you can give him.

A child whose fear stems from a fall or a scalding will have to be convinced anew that the tub is safe. A rubber mat should allay any fear of slipping; if need be, you can offer to help him in and out of the tub for a while. A fear of hot water can be more difficult to quiet, and you may have to resort to sponge baths until you can slowly reintroduce the idea of bathing in the tub.

If your child is afraid of being sucked down the drain, the easiest solution is to wait until he is out of the tub before pulling the plug. Reassure him that he is much too big to slip down the drain. If you like, you can demonstrate this by draining the tub while his toys are still in it. Once he sees that his toys, which are much smaller than he is, will not fit, perhaps he will understand that neither will he.

Dealing with shampoos

Even children who love their baths may dislike having their hair shampooed. For some youngsters, it is the thought of having to close their eyes that makes shampooing so unpleasant. Others may simply dislike having water poured over their heads. Many more are understandably scared of the soap stinging their eyes.

This last complaint is the easiest to relieve. Simply make certain to use a mild, nonirritating shampoo. In dealing with other concerns, you can try using a dry washcloth to cover the child's eyes during rinsing. Or you could outfit her with swimming goggles or a diving mask, which might even make it all fun. A rubber visor might help, too. Try shampooing your child's hair by having her lie on her back with an inch or two of water in the tub and pouring the rinse water over her head in a way that keeps it off her face. Some parents find that a hand-held spray helps to keep soapy water out of a child's eyes. When you are done, be sure to tell her how clean and shiny her hair looks.

Aside from appearance and general cleanliness, shampoos are helpful in controlling a scaly inflammation of the scalp known as cradle cap. Do not be deceived by the name; children of any age, not merely infants, may be subject to cradle cap, which is a childhood form of dandruff. If cradle cap is a problem, ask your doctor to recommend a specially formulated dandruff shampoo.

Combing and brushing

Until they learn what it can do for their appearance, most youngsters tend to regard combing and brushing as a bother. But it is

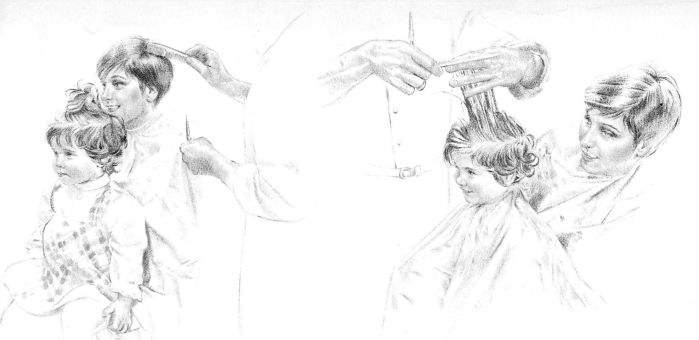

an important part of a child's grooming, and you should make it a point to give your toddler's hair a good brushing every day.

To make it easier on yourself and your youngster, use a children's conditioner on her hair after shampooing; it will minimize the fuss over snarls and tangles. And you can make a game out of it, perhaps by pretending that you both are at the beauty parlor, where she is having her hair dried and styled "just like a big girl."

As she grows older, she should be encouraged to care for her own hair each morning. Buy a comb and brush sized for little hands and hang a small mirror low on the wall so she can see herself. Gentle reminders when you notice that she has not brushed and praise when she has will keep her going, until before long a brisk brushing will be second nature.

Haircuts
Sometime before your child is 18 months old, you will have to decide who is going to cut his hair, you or a barber. If you opt for a barber, spend a little time finding someone who has a way with children. That kind of good reputation gets around, so other parents are likely to have a recommendation. With luck, your first trip to the barbershop will go smoothly, and your youngster will be looking forward to future visits with his new friend.

If you decide to cut your child's hair yourself — and many parents do it very well indeed — just remember that nothing succeeds like patience. It is going to take awhile, and you will need your youngster's cooperation. Have enough books for him to look at, or let him watch TV. Some parents let their toddler leave the chair occasionally to romp around for a few minutes. And one clever mother lured her child into the chair by telling him, "Instead of napping today, you can stay up with me and get a haircut," thereby instantly transforming a chore into a treat.

Washing hands
As your youngster explores the world around him, his busy little hands will find their way into all manner of interesting mess.

Alas, mess means germs, so one of the first things you will want to teach him is how to wash his hands properly.

In the beginning, you will have to take your child's hands in yours and go through the washing procedure for him. But by the time he is two years old, he should start making the effort on his own — an effort you should encourage, no matter how inefficient he may be at first. Naturally, he will learn more quickly if you make it easy for him to reach the sink, so keep a stool in the bathroom. And since a big bar of soap is often too cumbersome, you will want to supply some minibars of soap or better still, a bottle of liquid soap with a push-pump. Children love to squirt out the soap, and injecting a bit of fun into a routine is usually a good idea. Be sure to keep a towel handy on a low rack; your child will appreciate being able to dry himself off with as little help as possible. And by all means, praise his efforts by telling him what a big boy he is and how well he has done.

It is important to teach your youngster how to use the faucets correctly from the start in order to avoid accidental scalding. Make certain that he always turns on the cold water first and then the hot, until the tap water is comfortably warm. As a precaution while your child is learning about faucets, keep your water-heater temperature set at a maximum of 125° F.

Trimming nails Bathtime is the best time to trim your child's fingernails and toenails, since they will be softer and easier to cut then. And when the job is all done she will have a sense of neatness as well as cleanliness. Use a special blunt-tipped scissor or nail clipper designed for children and trim straight across, just below the top of the finger. If your toddler does not want to sit still while having her nails done, try distracting her with a toy. Or make a game of it by singing a little song or counting each small finger and toe as you go along.

Care of the teeth The foundation for good dental care should be laid as soon as your infant gets her first tooth. Those baby teeth are important to her speech and her eating habits, and they are critical to the proper formation and placement of her permanent teeth. A decayed baby tooth that must be removed can cause nearby teeth to move into the empty space; her permanent teeth could come in crowded and misshapen as a result. But such problems are easy to guard against. Preventive care includes proper diet, careful brushing with a toothpaste containing fluoride, which is recommended as an added safeguard against cavities, and checkups by the dentist beginning at the age of two or three. If your

Show your child how to brush and floss his teeth by demonstrating the technique shown here, as he looks into a mirror. Use a small, soft child's brush and replace it as soon as the bristles are worn or frayed. This may be every three or four months, since preschoolers often chew on bristles or stroke improperly when learning.

home's water supply is not fluoridated, ask your dentist about using a fluoride supplement as well.

Your youngster is likely to have several primary teeth by the time she reaches her first birthday. At least once each day, and more often if possible, you should wipe off her teeth and gums with a piece of gauze or a damp washcloth. This will remove any deposits of harmful plaque, which could cause decay and subsequent loss of a tooth if allowed to accumulate. Take care, too, that you do not let your toddler fall asleep while sucking on a bottle of milk, juice or some other sweet drink; the liquid could pool around her teeth and gums, and in league with the bacteria found in dental plaque, result in a particularly damaging form of decay known as nursing-bottle mouth.

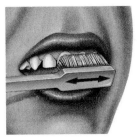

To get at the plaque hidden on chewing surfaces and the outsides of teeth, hold the brush horizontally at a 45 degree angle to the gumline, then brush gently back and forth with short strokes.

Teaching your child to brush When your child is two years old — or perhaps a bit older, depending on her level of motor development — you will want to start teaching her how to brush her own teeth. She should have a special toothbrush designed for baby teeth, with soft, end-rounded or polished bristles. You should lead her through the motions *(above)* the first few times. Then put a small amount of toothpaste on the brush and encourage her to try brushing her teeth on her own. If she seems to be concentrating more on sucking the toothpaste than brushing, however, let her use plain water at the beginning. Do not expect a young child to master tooth-brushing immediately; at this point, your aim is simply to establish the habit. If necessary, you can finish the job, but let her do as much as she can by herself. Teach her to be consistent about it; shuttle her off to brush after every meal, if possible, and certainly twice a day. By the age of four or five, she may be expertly brushing her teeth entirely on her own, though it is still a good idea for you to look in periodically to make sure that she is doing a thorough job.

To clean the inside surfaces of the front teeth, hold the toothbrush perpendicular to the gumline in a slightly tilted position. Stroke up and down with the front part of the brush.

Flossing to remove plaque from between the teeth is just as important for children as it is for adults, although it is probably beyond your youngster's abilities when she is very young, and you will have to do it for her. As she gains greater motor control, however, you will want to teach her to floss regularly, preferably twice a day, and at the very least before bedtime. Naturally, the lesson should be reinforced by your own good example. ⁘

To remove plaque, hold the floss taut and gently ease it between two teeth until it touches the gum. Curve the floss into a C shape and slide it up and down against the side of each tooth.

127

Learning to Get Dressed

By the age of one or two, most children have no trouble at all getting undressed on their own, since it is both easy and fun to wriggle out of pants and shirts. In fact, some youngsters seem to spend more time with their clothing off than they do with it on.

But getting dressed is another matter — and one with more than its share of frustration. As he grows older, your toddler may want to get dressed on his own, only to find that his little fingers are no match for an obstacle course of zippers, buttons and shoelaces. He may want to decide himself what to wear, only to hear you keep telling him this does not go with that or it is too cold today to wear a favorite pair of shorts. And he may feel that given a little time in the morning, he will eventually get the right shoe on the right foot, only to have you hurry him along because the carpool is waiting.

Eventually of course, zippers do get zipped and buttons buttoned; arms find their way into the appropriate sleeves and shirt fronts get sorted out from shirt backs, until by the age of four or five, most children are dressing themselves correctly. In another year or two, you can encourage your youngster to gather up his dirty clothes and put them in the laundry hamper, hang up clean clothes and put his shoes in the closet. Along the road to responsibility, however, your child will need your cooperation and help. By offering generous praise, storing his clothes where he can get at them and demonstrating the secrets of slipping into shoes and socks and pants and shirts, you can speed him on his way to this important new skill.

Choosing your child's wardrobe In selecting clothes for your child, keep a few simple guidelines in mind. Look for pants with stretch waistbands and self-lengthening cuffs, dresses with hems and seams that can be let out, and overalls with adjustable suspenders. Buy clothing that gives your toddler freedom of movement and will be easy for her to get on and off by herself. And be sure to take into account your child's personality and desires. Do not, for example, insist that she wear frilly dresses when you know how much she loves to play outdoors. It is also a good idea to give your youngster some say in selecting her clothing when you go shopping. Pick several outfits that you can live with, then allow her to make the final selection. Her first choice may not necessarily be your first choice, but her pride and self-confidence will benefit from having had the opportunity to choose.

Buying shoes The best shoes for a child are those that most closely simulate his bare feet. Buy shoes that are shaped like his foot, not pointy. And be sure that they are comfortably flexible; you should be able to bend the soles easily with your hand. Be careful, too, that the shoes are not too snug; young feet do not need support, but they do need plenty of room for growth — about half an inch at the toes is recommended. The shoes can either be high top or not; the argument in favor of high-top shoes is that they are more likely to stay on than such styles as low-top sneakers and sandals — at least at early ages. Children of all ages should wear footwear made of leather, canvas or other breathable materials, never plastic, which can lead to juvenile plantar dermatosis — a skin inflammation caused by insufficient air circulation.

Getting into coats and jackets need not be a struggle when you teach your child this little trick: Have him lay his coat on the floor with the front side up and the zipper open. Next, have him kneel at the collar and slip his arms through the sleeves. Then he can stand up, flip the coat over his head and — presto! — he has it on.

Until your child is about two years old, she will need you to get her dressed each morning. But gradually, as her motor skills increase, you should let her take on more of the responsibility for dressing herself. Offer help whenever necessary, but allow her to do as much as she can on her own.

You can begin by storing her clothes in accessible locations. High bureau drawers and out-of-reach clothing bars only force her to ask for your assistance; instead, keep her clothing in lower drawers and lower the clothing bar in the closet or install pegs on her bedroom wall at her own height.

When it comes to the actual dressing, you should provide minimal hands-on assistance and maximum encouragement. Even toddlers can learn to step into the circles of trouser legs after you have rolled them up and laid them on the floor. Once her feet are in both legs, show her how to bend down, take hold of the tops of the pants and pull them up. At this early age, she will still need your help to get the pants over her diaper, but at least she is participating and learning more each morning. In the same manner, you can pull her socks on as far as her heels, then encourage her to tug them up the rest of the way.

When your child is a little older, you can show her how to lay a pair of pants out flat on the floor, then sit at the waistband and slip her feet through the correct legs before pulling the pants up. A pullover shirt should be laid flat on the bed, front side down, so the child can pick it up at the bottom and slip it over her head herself. By now, socks should be easy to manage, especially if you buy tube socks so there are no heels to confuse her.

Shoes present several problems, not the least of which is telling the left shoe from the right. You can help by showing your child how to line up the shoes on the floor with the toes curving in toward each other, then stand behind them and slip her right and left feet into the appropriate shoes. If you wish, you can temporarily postpone teaching the ins and outs of shoelaces by buying shoes with hook-and-loop fasteners, such as Velcro® tape. But by the age of six, with patient instruction, most children are able to master the mysteries of the bow knot.

Zippers, buttons and snaps are a challenge for a young child's developing fine-motor skills, so give your youngster plenty of opportunities to practice. You can start the zipper going and let her pull the slide up the rest of the way. For early buttoning efforts, choose large, easy-to-manipulate buttons. Show your child how to fasten snaps between her thumb and forefinger.

Inevitably, as your child takes on more of the responsibility for dressing herself, she will want to choose what to wear on certain days. This is likely to result in some outlandish color and pattern combinations. That need not bother you at these ages, but if it does, you might try offering her a choice between two coordinated outfits. In that way, you will reduce the chance of a garish combination, while still gratifying your child's sense of control by leaving the choice itself up to her — just as you did when shopping. It is also a good idea to compliment your youngster when she does pick a shirt and pants that match properly, thus reinforcing the message that certain colors and patterns look nice together.

A two-year-old's natural swings between dependence and independence give rise to some vexing behavior as he learns how to dress himself. He may, for example, insist on dressing himself one day, then demand your help the following day, only to refuse to get dressed at all the very next. Or he may let you know what he thinks about the whole thing by gleefully scampering away the

A good way to help your child pick out his own clothes for the day and dress himself is to organize his dresser: Tape drawings or cutouts to the drawers showing where different kinds of clothes are kept. Words can come later, as his interest in reading grows. Add to his sense of responsibility by providing a small ladder where he can hang jackets and fold pants, sweaters and other garments that may be worn more than once.

moment you remove his pajamas. The best way to handle such situations is by focusing on the underlying plea for attention. In refusing to dress himself, he may only be saying that while cherishing his growing independence, he still misses the times when you babied him. A little pampering may do him a world of good at this point, so offer to help him get dressed; in all likelihood, the helping hand will make him more cooperative. When your youngster insists on doing everything himself, let him; if he needs your help, he will usually ask. Likewise, a child who runs away during dressing wants you to chase him. But since he probably will not want to get dressed once you catch him — and since his defiance may only spark your anger — you would do better to ignore him and simply wait until he is ready to get dressed. If time is pressing, however, your best strategy is to put the child's clothes on him gently but firmly and tell him that this is how it must be.

Even more frustrating to some parents is the child who can dress himself but takes forever to do it, or the youngster who cannot quite make up his mind whether to wear the blue shirt or the red one. Here again the solution is the obvious one: As long as there is no hurry, do not hurry him; he will get dressed in his own good time. On the other hand, if there is a school bus to catch or you just cannot bear another morning of indecision, try helping him choose the next day's clothes before going to bed. Or if there are brothers or sisters in the family, turn the morning dressing ritual into a contest to see who gets dressed first. The spirit of competition may hasten your dawdler along.

Coats and cold weather Finally, there is the youngster who stubbornly refuses to put on a coat before going out to play. Before getting upset, remember that an active child has less need for heavy clothing because his body is churning up enough heat to keep him warm. Moreover, many children dislike the bulkiness of a winter-weight coat. In such cases, a compromise may be in order. You might allow him to wear a sweater or jacket on the condition that if he feels cold he will come in and get a coat. Or you might try layering the youngster's clothing so that he can remove a sweater or jacket if he feels too warm.

One novel solution is to install a thermometer near a window and let it decide whether or not a coat is needed. Choose and mark a minimum temperature ahead of time, which your child can read for himself. Any resentment the youngster might feel at having to don a coat might then be directed at the inanimate thermometer, not you. ⁙

Managing Mealtimes

Until your child is a year or so old, mealtimes may be relatively orderly affairs, with the baby strapped into his high chair and Mommy or Daddy controlling the spoon. But somewhere around the end of their first year, most children show an interest in feeding themselves. Messy as it is certain to be, now is the time to let your toddler start developing these important self-help skills. Equip him with a spoon, a dish with rounded sides and a cup with a lid; then spread some paper on the floor beneath the high chair and let him go to it.

At first, the child will eat with his fingers or use them to transfer food to his spoon. No doubt he will mash, crumble, dribble, spit and fling food — simply for the fun of it. You may fear he will starve to death because so little actually gets into his stomach. But do not fret. With encouragement, he will get the hang of using a spoon by about 16 months of age.

When he is about two, you can introduce him to a fork; one with blunt tines and a spoonlike bowl is best. Soon he will learn to maneuver peas onto his fork or spoon by pushing them against the sides of the bowl. By the time he is three, let him try a small, blunt table knife. He will swiftly learn to smear jam onto bread, though he may be five before he is able to cut meat.

Minimizing mealtime problems It may come as a surprise, but at the same time your toddler is showing some proficiency in feeding herself, she is likely to show less interest in food. Between the ages of two and three, her growth rate may slow temporarily and appetite may decrease. By then, too, she will be testing her growing independence — along with her likes and dislikes — and your ever louder exhortations to eat what you have put before her are likely to result in a stalemate.

You can spare everybody mealtime aggravation by not insisting that your child eat everything you want her to eat. Recognize the fact that your youngster's taste buds and nutritional needs are different from your own and allow her to express her preferences. And do not worry: So long as her overall diet is wholesome, it will not matter if she merely nibbles for days at a time or insists on having the same kind of sandwich for lunch every day for weeks on end. By remaining calm, you will let your youngster know that refusing food or acting up at the table is not the way to capture your attention.

This does not mean, of course, that you should tolerate all manner of obstinacy and mischief at the table. On the contrary, as a parent you must set certain limits. If a child plays endlessly with food, feel free to take her plate away. If she misbehaves

When your toddler is very young, you will want to fill his plate for him. But as he becomes more adept with his hands, encourage him to serve himself at the table. This will not only help teach him about manners and sharing but also will give him practice in making choices.

severely during a meal, send her to her room; isolation is often the best way to deal with such situations.

Table manners and helping

By the time your child is three, he will be ready to learn some table manners. Many children this age are intrigued by formality and rituals and will respond with enthusiasm to such guidelines as "elbows off the table" and "one bite of food at a time" if they are introduced in a pleasant rather than a heavy-handed way.

Naturally, the best way to demonstrate table etiquette is through your own example, together with a bit of instruction now and then and the occasional reminder to remember "please" and "thank you" or not to talk with a full mouth.

Many children enjoy helping out in the kitchen, and older children especially should be encouraged to lend a hand. Even toddlers can be enlisted to help by cracking eggs with a parent's assistance or by stirring batter. Older children can be taught how to set the table and clear away the plates after a meal. By the time he is four, your child can make his own peanut-butter-and-jelly sandwiches and pour his own drinks. Spills are inevitable; just mop them up without scolding.

Dining out

Taking your little one to a fancy restaurant is not a good idea until he is old enough to sit through a meal without disrupting it and disturbing others. Until then, it is better to patronize family establishments where the unpredictable behavior of children is more likely to be tolerated. When you do go out, go early — when the restaurant is less crowded and will offer the child fewer mealtime distractions. And be prepared to deal with hunger or boredom: You can use bread sticks or other finger foods to keep your child occupied while you are waiting to be served. ⁂

Teaching Safety Sense

As your baby learns to walk and her innate curiosity leads her afield, she is bound to pick up a few bumps and bruises here and there. Painful though they can be, these little accidents are one of the ways in which your toddler learns to recognize her limits. They are mistakes like any other mistakes and through them she will learn what is and is not safe.

Naturally, you want to keep your child from harm. But by being overprotective and trying to shield her from every minor tumble and scrape, you will only make her more fearful and dependent. It is far better to accept the fact that accidents do happen and to concentrate on minimizing the number of serious ones by instilling in your child a sense of safety to temper the impetuousness that comes with her growing independence.

Warning of hazards   From the start, warn your child of dangers by telling her "No," or "Hot," or "Don't touch," whenever she gets too close to a particular area or encounters a perilous situation. You need not shout, but be firm. In time, she will associate the words with the hazards and steer clear. Also take advantage of mishaps that might have been avoided by calmly pointing out what caused the accident and how to be more careful next time. As your child grows older, you will want to set a strong example of sensible safety. Children from two to six love to imitate their parents, and it is essential that they have the right things to imitate. When you use a faucet, for example, do so properly so your child learns to turn it on gently — and then to turn it off when she is through. And be aware, of course, that many household items and appliances are simply not for little hands; it is best to keep all potentially dangerous tools and materials well out of reach. This is particularly important in regard to household cleansers and the contents of the medicine cabinet.

An older child, too, will start playing outside more frequently: in your yard, at a friend's or perhaps at a local playground — and without you around to stand guard over her every second. She must learn not to wander away and understand that such places as roads, railroad tracks and building sites are strictly off limits. Be sure to explain why; you do not want her natural curiosity to tempt her to find out on her own.

Safety in the car   Auto accidents are the leading cause of death and serious injury among children. Authorities estimate that 90 percent of the deaths and 70 percent of the injuries could have been avoided had the children been strapped into safety seats or wearing seat belts. All 50 states now have mandatory seat-belt laws for chil-

A convertible safety seat can be used to hold an infant safely in a reclining, rear-facing position, and later it can be adjusted upright and faced forward to hold an older child who weighs up to about 40 pounds.

dren. But it is just common sense to see that your youngster is properly restrained at all times while traveling in the car. And do not relax this rule even for those short trips to your local supermarket or shopping mall; those same bitter statistics show that 80 percent of all fatalities occur within a few blocks of home at speeds of 40 miles per hour or less.

Most car seats fall into one of two categories: the safety seat and the booster seat. Which one is right for your child depends on how big he is, while the seat's effectiveness depends on how closely you follow the manufacturer's instructions. In general, infants and children weighing less than 40 pounds should be properly buckled into a safety seat that is anchored in place with the car's seat belt *(above)*. A toddler or older child can use a booster seat in conjunction with a seat belt *(right)*. If the child is tall enough to do without the booster seat, a shoulder-lap belt will suffice *(below)*. You may need to tuck the shoulder strap behind the child if it crosses the neck or face. The safest place for a child of any age to sit is always in the back seat, preferably in the middle.

In addition to protecting your youngster, buckling up offers the bonus of better behavior in the car. Since your youngster is securely and comfortably strapped into his seat, there is no opportunity for him to stand up, jump around or generally turn the car into a playground on wheels.

There are some other precautions to keep in mind when traveling with children. You should make sure you buckle up yourself, both for your own protection and that of the other occupants in the car, as well as to set a good example for your children. Keep the car doors locked while driving and do not let children put their heads, arms or hands out of the car's windows. Establish behavior rules that will minimize distractions to the driver, and on long trips, stop every hour or two to allow your youngsters to run around and burn off excess energy.

While the playground is always a source of great fun for children, it can also be a very dangerous place. The swings, the monkey bars and jungle gyms, the slides, crawl-through pipes and seesaws are marvelous for exercising young muscles and imaginations. But enjoying the playground safely requires some

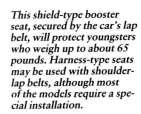

This shield-type booster seat, secured by the car's lap belt, will protect youngsters who weigh up to about 65 pounds. Harness-type seats may be used with shoulder-lap belts, although most of the models require a special installation.

When your child weighs more than 40 pounds, she can probably use a shoulder-lap restraint. Make sure that the belt buckles across the hips, not the abdomen.

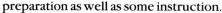

preparation as well as some instruction.

Make sure that your youngster is wearing sneakers or shoes with nonskid soles before she heads off to the playground. And her clothing should be more or less form-fitting, without long, loose folds or sashes that might catch on playground equipment.

Assure yourself that the playground is maintained. Bolts and screws should be securely fastened with no exposed parts to snag children or their clothing. There should be no sharp edges or exposed rusted metal; rings should be larger than 10 inches or smaller than five inches to reduce the chance that a child might ensnare her head; any S hooks should be closed to prevent pinched fingers; and all equipment should be anchored in concrete. If you notice anything amiss, you should notify the appropriate authorities.

But no matter how safe a playground may appear, preschoolers should always be under adult supervision. Teach your child to use playground equipment only as it was designed to be used. She should sit in the middle of a swing seat and avoid standing in front of a slide or swing. She should also hang on with both hands when climbing, swinging or seesawing, and she should be discouraged from leaping to the ground from high levels. Playground manners are important, too. If she learns to take turns, she is less likely to get in shoving matches or fights.

Good street-crossing habits should be drilled into your youngster from the very start. He should learn to cross only at crosswalks and always to stop at the curb and look both ways before stepping into the roadway. Warn, too, against darting from between parked cars or running after a ball that has rolled into the street.

Tricycles and bicycles

Tricycles and bicycles are favorite toys because of the marvelous sense of speed and mobility they provide. But therein lies the danger, as well. Indoors, it will not do for your youngster to race his tricycle around where there are sharp table corners to catch little heads, or stairs to tumble down. Outside, he should not be tempted to compete with traffic; you should make sure that he rides only on sidewalks or bike paths or in the safety of a backyard, driveway or park — never on streets. Since most tricycles lack brakes, your youngster should also learn to avoid hills, curbs, steps and other such obstacles. The same goes for bike riders. Even at the lofty age of six, children should generally be restricted to parks and sidewalks. If you do permit your child to use the street, perhaps in your company or under other protected circumstances, make sure he understands that he should stay as far to the right as possible and obey all signs and signals.

Street sense Automobile traffic represents one of the biggest dangers for children — afoot as well as on wheels. Active toddlers and preschoolers are impetuous creatures and must be watched closely anywhere around traffic. Make it a firm rule from the start that you always hold onto your child's hand while crossing a street or a parking lot. Never assume that he will stay placidly at your side. You may want to teach your youngster that the curb is a safety line, and that it is not to be crossed except in the company of Mommy or Daddy or some other responsible older person. Eventually, you will want to prepare him for the day he crosses on his own by teaching him about traffic lights, crosswalks, safety zones and such. But under no circumstances should a child under the age of six be allowed to cross a street alone.

Stores and strangers A trip to the shopping mall can be a mind-expanding experience for your youngster, but it can turn into a nightmare for you both if she happens to drift away and get lost. As you go about your business, keep your little one in the child's seat of a shopping cart or bring along your own stroller. Having your toddler in a secure place will make it much easier for you to shop and will still allow her to explore with her eyes — if not with her feet. Even after your child has outgrown the stroller and walks around on her own, keep her in your sight at all times in shopping centers and other public places. Do teach her to repeat her full name and address and your telephone number, however, in case she accidentally becomes separated from you.

At the proper stage, usually around the age of three, you will want to teach her about strangers. Begin by explaining to her that a stranger is someone — an adult or a considerably older child — whom she does not know well, and that not every person who speaks nicely to her is a friend. Warn her never to go in or near a stranger's car, to accept gifts or candy from strangers or to go inside a strange house. It is a good idea to avoid dressing your child in personalized clothing, since she is more likely to respond to people who call her by name.

Finally, be sure your youngster understands that no one has the right to touch her without her permission — not even a relative or a person she knows as a friend. Explain to her that she should tell you right away if anyone touches her, asks her to keep a secret, threatens her in any way or does anything else that makes her feel uncomfortable or scared. ❖

Bibliography

BOOKS

Ames, Louise Bates, and Frances L. Ilg:
Your Five-Year-Old: Sunny and Serene. New York: Delta Books, 1979.
Your Four-Year-Old: Wild and Wonderful. New York: Delta Books, 1976.
Your Three-Year-Old: Friend or Enemy. New York: Delta Books, 1976.
Your Two-Year-Old: Terrible or Tender. New York: Delta Books, 1976.

Ames, Louise Bates, Frances L. Ilg and Carol Chase Haber, *Your One-Year-Old: The Fun-Loving, Fussy 12-to 24-Month-Old.* New York: Delta Books, 1982.

Baer, Melvin, J., *Growth and Maturation: An Introduction to Physical Development.* Cambridge, Mass.: Howard A. Doyle, 1973.

Bailey, Rebecca Anne, and Elsie Carter Burton, *The Dynamic Self: Activities to Enhance Infant Development.* St. Louis: C. V. Mosby, 1982.

Beck, M. Susan, *Baby Talk: How Your Child Learns to Speak.* New York: New American Library, 1979.

Behrman, Richard E., M.D., and Victor C. Vaughan III, M.D., *Nelson Textbook of Pediatrics.* Philadelphia: W. B. Saunders, 1983.

Block, Susan Diamond, *Me and I'm Great: Physical Education for Children Three through Eight.* Minneapolis, Minn.: Burgess Publishing, 1977.

Boston Children's Hospital with Susan Baker, M.D., and Roberta R. Henry, *Parents' Guide to Nutrition: Healthy Eating from Birth through Adolescence.* Reading, Mass.: Addison-Wesley, 1986.

Boston Children's Medical Center, and Elizabeth M. Gregg, *What to Do When There's Nothing to Do.* Boston: Dell Books, 1968.

Bowerman, Melissa, "The Acquisition of Complex Sentences." In *Language Acquisition: Studies in First Language Development,* ed. by Paul Fletcher and Michael Garman. New York: Cambridge University Press, 1979.

Brody, Jane, *Jane Brody's Nutrition Book.* New York: Bantam Books, 1981.

Buchenholz, Gretchen, et. al., *Teach Your Child with Games.* New York: Simon & Schuster, 1984.

Burton, Elsie Carter, *Physical Activities for the Developing Child.* Springfield, Ill.: Charles C. Thomas, 1980.

Burtt, Kent Garland, *Smart Times: A Parent's Guide to Quality Time with Preschoolers.* New York: Harper & Row, 1984.

Caplan, Theresa, and Frank Caplan:
The Early Childhood Years: The 2- to 6-Year-Old. New York: Bantam Books, 1983.
The Second Twelve Months of Life: A Kaleidoscope of Growth. New York: Grosset & Dunlap, 1979.

Childhood Medical Guide, by the Editors of Time-Life Books (Successful Parenting Series). Alexandria, Va.: Time-Life Books, 1986.

Chinn, Peggy L., *Child Health Maintenance: Concepts in Family-Centered Care.* St. Louis: C. V. Mosby, 1979.

Coggins, Truman E., and Robert L. Carpenter, "Introduction to the Area of Language Development." In *The Developmental Resource: Behavioral Sequences for Assessment and Program Planning,* Vol. 2, by Marilyn A. Cohen and Pamela J. Gross. New York: Grune & Stratton, 1979.

Cohen, Marilyn A., and Pamela J. Gross, *The Developmental Resource.* Vols. 1 and 2. New York: Grune & Stratton, 1979.

Corbin, Charles B., ed., *A Textbook of Motor Development.* Dubuque, Iowa: William C. Brown, 1980.

Cratty, Bryant J., *Perceptual and Motor Development in Infants and Children.* Englewood Cliffs, N.J.: Prentice-Hall, 1986.

Crystal, David, *Listen to Your Child: A Parent's Guide to Children's Language.* New York: Viking, 1986.

Curtis, Sandra R., *The Joy of Movement.* New York: Teachers College Press, 1982.

Dauer, Victor Paul, *Essential Movement Experiences for Preschool and Primary Children.* Minneapolis: Burgess, 1972.

DeLorenzo, Lorisa, and Robert John DeLorenzo, M.D., *Total Child Care: From Birth to Age Five.* New York: Doubleday, 1982.

de Villiers, Jill G., and Peter A. de Villiers:
Early Language. Cambridge, Mass.: Harvard University Press, 1979.
Language Acquisition. Cambridge, Mass.: Harvard University Press, 1978.

Diagram Group, *Child's Body.* New York: Paddington Press Ltd., 1977.

Einon, Dorothy, *Play With A Purpose: Learning Games for Children Six Weeks to Ten Years.* New York: Pantheon Books, 1985.

Endres, Jeannette Brakhane, and Robert E. Rockwell, *A Parents' Guide to Kids' Nutrition.* St. Louis: C. V. Mosby, 1983.

Engstrom, Georgianna, ed., *The Significance of the Young Child's Motor Development.* Washington: National Association for the Education of Young Children, 1971.

Espenschade, Anna S., and Helen M. Eckert, *Motor Development.* Columbus, Ohio: Charles E. Merrill, 1980.

Fisher, John J., *Infants & Toddlers: Endless Play Ideas That Make Learning Fun.* New York: Putnam, 1986.

Gallahue, David L.:
Developmental Movement Experiences for Children. New York: John Wiley & Sons, 1982.
Developmental Play Equipment for Home and School. New York: John Wiley & Sons, 1975.
Motor Development and Movement Experiences for Young Children (3-7). New York: John Wiley & Sons, 1976.

Garvey, Catherine, *Children's Talk.* Cambridge, Mass.: Harvard University Press, 1984.

Goldberg, Sally, *Growing with Games.* Ann Arbor, Mich.: The University of Michigan Press, 1985.

Gordon, Ira J., *Baby Learning Through Baby Play: A Parent's Guide for the First Two Years.* New York: St. Martin's Press, 1970.

Gordon, Ira J., Barry Guinagh and R. Emile Jester, *Child Learning Through Child Play: Learning Activities for Two and Three Year Olds.* New York: St. Martin's Press, 1972.

Grasselli, Rose N., and Priscilla A. Hegner, *Playful Parenting: Games to Help Your Infants and Toddlers Grow Physically, Mentally & Emotionally.* New York: Putnam, 1981.

Hardyment, Christina, *Dream Babies: Child Care from Locke to Spock.* New York: Oxford University Press, 1984.

Herriot, Peter, et. al, eds., *Let's Learn: Play and Games.* London: Mitchell Beazley, 1982.

Holzman, Mathilda, *The Language of Children: Development in Home and School.* Englewood Cliffs, N.J.: Prentice-Hall, 1983.

Johnson, Thomas R., M.D., William M. Moore, M.D., and James E. Jeffries, eds., *Children are Different: Developmental Physiology.* Columbus, Ohio: Ross Laboratories, 1978.

Kaluger, George, and Meriem Fair Kaluger, *Human Development: The Span of Life.* St. Louis: C. V. Mosby, 1979.

Karnes, Merle B., *You and Your Small Wonder: Activities for Parents and Toddlers on the Go.* Circle Pines, Minn.: American Guidance Service, 1982.

Kelly, Noeline Thompson, and Brian John Kelly, *Physical Education for Pre-School and Primary Grades.* Springfield, Ill.: Charles C. Thomas, 1985.

Krogman, Wilton Marion, *Child Growth.* Ann Arbor, Mich.: University of Michigan Press, 1972.

Lambert-Lagacé, Louise, *Feeding Your Child: From Infancy to Six Years Old.* New York: Beaufort Books, 1982.

Lansky, Vicki, *Practical Parenting: Toilet Training.* New York: Bantam Books, 1984.

Leitch, Susan M., *A Child Learns to Speak: A Guide for Parents and Teachers of Preschool Children.* Springfield, Ill.: Charles C. Thomas, 1977.

Levine, Melvin D., M.D., et. al., *Developmental Behavioral Pediatrics.* Philadelphia: W. B. Saunders, 1983.

Lord, Catherine, "Psychopathology in Early Development." In *The Young Child: Reviews of Research,* Vol. 3, ed. by Shirley G. Moore and Catherine R. Cooper. Washington: National Association for the Education of Young Children, 1982.

Lowrey, George H., M.D., *Growth and Development*

of Children. Chicago: Year Book Medical Publishers, 1978.

Lynch-Fraser, Diane, *Dance Play: Creative Movement for Very Young Children.* New York: Walker, 1982.

Mack, Alison, *Toilet Learning: The Picture Book Technique for Children and Parents.* Boston: Little, Brown, 1978.

Magee, Patricia Boggia, and Marilyn Reichwald Ornstein, *Come With Us To Playgroup: A Handbook for Parents and Teachers of Young Children.* Englewood Cliffs, N.J.: Prentice-Hall, 1981.

Marlow, Dorothy R., *Textbook of Pediatric Nursing.* Philadelphia: W. B. Saunders, 1977.

Marzollo, Jean, and Janice Lloyd, *Learning through Play.* New York: Harper Colophon Books, 1972.

Michaelis, Bill, and Dolores Michaelis, *Learning Through Noncompetitive Activities and Play.* Palo Alto, Calif.: David S. Lake, 1977.

Miller, Jon, David E. Yoder and Richard Schiefelbusch, eds. *Contemporary Issues in Language Intervention.* ASHA Reports 12. Rockville, Md.: The American Speech-Language-Hearing Association, 1983.

Miller, Karen, *Things To Do With Toddlers and Twos.* Boston: Telshare Publishing, 1984.

Mussen, Paul Henry, et. al., *Child Development and Personality.* New York: Harper & Row, 1984.

Nelms, Bobbie Crew, and Ruth G. Mullins, *Growth and Development: A Primary Health Care Approach.* Englewood Cliffs, N.J.: Prentice-Hall, 1982.

Owens, Robert E., Jr., *Language Development: An Introduction.* Columbus, Ohio: Charles E. Merrill, 1984.

Prudden, Suzy, *Suzy Prudden's Exercise Program for Young Children.* New York: Workman, 1983.

Reich, Peter A., *Language Development.* Englewood Cliffs, N.J.: Prentice-Hall, 1986.

Riggs, Maida L., *Jump to Joy: Helping Children Grow through Active Play.* Englewood Cliffs, N.J.: Prentice-Hall, 1980.

Riggs, Maida L., ed., *Movement Education for Preschool Children.* Reston, Va.: American Alliance for Health, Physical Education, Recreation and Dance, 1980.

Rubin, Richard R., et. al., *Your Preschooler: Ages Three and Four.* New York: Macmillan, 1982.

Rubin, Richard R., John J. Fisher III and Susan G. Doering, *Your Toddler: Ages One and Two.*

New York: Macmillan, 1980.

Samuels, Mike, M.D., and Nancy Samuels:
The Well Baby Book. New York: Summit Books, 1979.
The Well Child Book. New York: Summit Books, 1982.

Scarr, Sandra, Richard A. Weinberg and Ann Levine, *Understanding Development.* New York: Harcourt Brace Jovanovich, 1986.

Schoedler, James, *Physical Skills for Young Children.* New York: Macmillan, 1973.

Sher, Barbara, *Moving Right Along.* Whitethorn, Calif.: Bright Baby Books, 1985.

Sinclair, David, M.D., *Human Growth After Birth.* New York: Oxford University Press, 1985.

Skinner, Louise, *Motor Development in the Preschool Years.* Springfield, Ill.: Charles C. Thomas, 1979.

Smith, David W., M.D., *Growth and Its Disorders.* Philadelphia: W. B. Saunders, 1977.

Sparling, Joseph, and Isabelle Lewis, *Learningames for Threes and Fours: A Guide to Adult/Child Play.* New York: Walker, 1984.

Sullivan, Molly, *Feeling Strong, Feeling Free: Movement Exploration for Young Children.* Washington: National Association for the Education of Young Children, 1982.

Sullivan, S. Adams, *The Quality Time Almanac: A Sourcebook of Ideas and Activities for Parents and Kids.* New York: Doubleday, 1986.

Tackett, Jo Joyce Marie, and Mabel Hunsberger, *Family-Centered Care of Children and Adolescents: Nursing Concepts in Child Health.* Philadelphia: W. B. Saunders, 1981.

Tanner, J. M., *Foetus Into Man: Physical Growth from Conception to Maturity.* Cambridge, Mass.: Harvard University Press, 1978.

Waechter, Eugenia H., and Florence G. Blake, *Nursing Care of Children.* Philadelphia: J. B. Lippincott, 1976.

Watson, Ernest H., M.D., and George H. Lowrey, M.D., *Growth and Development of Children.* Chicago: Year Book Medical, 1962.

Weeks, Thelma E., *Born to Talk.* Rowley, Mass.: Newbury House, 1979.

Wells, Gordon, *Language Development in the Preschool Years.* New York: Cambridge University Press, 1985.

Whaley, Lucille F., and Donna L. Wong, *Nursing Care of Infants and Children.* St. Louis:

C. V. Mosby, 1983.

Williams, Harriet G., *Perceptual and Motor Development.* Englewood Cliffs, N.J.: Prentice-Hall, 1983.

Winick, Myron, M.D., *Growing Up Healthy: A Parent's Guide to Good Nutrition.* New York: William Morrow, 1982.

Zaichkowsky, Leonard D., Linda B. Zaichkowsky and Thomas J. Martinek, *Growth and Development: The Child and Physical Activity.* St. Louis: C. V. Mosby, 1980.

PERIODICALS

Garrard, Kay, "Perspectives on Child Talk." *Pediatrics for Parents,* October 1986.

Gelman, David, "The Mouths of Babes." *Newsweek,* December 15, 1986.

Gottwald, Sheryl Ridener, Peggy Goldbach and Audrey H. Isack, "Stuttering: Prevention and Detection." *Young Children,* November 1985.

Sander, Eric K., "When Are Speech Sounds Learned?" *Journal of Speech and Hearing Disorders,* February 1972.

Wedmore, Suellen, "When to Worry About Your Child's Speech." *Mothering,* Summer 1986.

OTHER PUBLICATIONS

American Dental Association, "Your Child's Teeth." Chicago, Ill.: Bureau of Health Education and Audiovisual Services, 1983.

Glover, M. Elayne, Jodi L. Preminger and Anne R. Sanford, *E-Lap: The Early Learning Accomplishment Profile for Developmentally Young Children.* Winston Salem, N.C.: Kaplan Press, 1978.

"Guide to Good Eating." Rosemont, Ill.: National Dairy Council, 1986.

"Guide to Wise Food Choices." Rosemont, Ill.: National Dairy Council, 1986.

Liebergott, Jacqueline, et. al., *Mainstreaming Preschoolers: Children with Speech and Language Impairments.* DHEW Publication No. (OHDS) 78-31113. Washington: U.S. Department of Health, Education, and Welfare, 1978.

"NCHS Growth Curves for Children: Birth-18 Years." DHEW Publication No. (PHS) 78-1650. Washington: U.S. Department of Health, Education, and Welfare, November 1977.

Sanford, Anne R., and Janet G. Zelman, *LAP: The Learning Accomplishment Profile.* Winston-Salem, N.C.: Kaplan Press, 1981.

Acknowledgments and Picture Credits

The index for this book was prepared by Louise Hedberg. The editors also thank Maida L. Riggs, Hadley, Mass.

The sources for the photographs and illustrations in this book are listed below. Credits from left to right are separated by semicolons; credits from top to bottom are separated by dashes.

Photographs. Cover: Joe Rubino. 7: Lucy Brown. 11, 12: Beecie Kupersmith. 39: Joe Rubino. 41: Susie Fitzhugh. 51-87: Joe Rubino. 109: Dan Cunningham. 110, 116: Beecie Kupersmith.

Illustrations. 8, 14: Donald Gates from photos by Beecie Kupersmith. 16, 17: Donald Gates from photo by Susanne Szasz. 18-21: John Drummond. 23, 25: Donald Gates from photos by Beecie Kupersmith. 29: William Hennessy. 31: Donald Gates from photo by Beecie Kupersmith. 32: Bill Burrows & Associate. 34-37: Bill Burrows & Associate from photos by Beecie Kupersmith. 42-49: Robert Hynes from photos by Beecie Kupersmith. 54-57: Marguerite E. Bell from photos by Joe Rubino. 60-63: Kathe Scherr from photos by Joe Rubino. 66-69: Marguerite E. Bell from photos by Joe Rubino. 72-75: Kathe Scherr from photos by Joe Rubino. 78-81: Marguerite E. Bell from photos by Joe Rubino. 82-85: William Hennessy. 88: Robert Hynes from photos by Jane Jordan. 90, 91: Robert Hynes from photos by Beecie Kupersmith. 93: William Westwood. 94, 95: William Hennessy. 97-105: Robert Hynes from photos by Beecie Kupersmith. 112-122: Donald Gates from photos by Beecie Kupersmith. 125: Donald Gates from photo by Jane Jordan. 127: Donald Gates from photo by Jane Jordan — William Westwood (3). 128-131: Donald Gates from photos by Beecie Kupersmith. 133: Donald Gates from photo by Jane Jordan. 135, 136: Donald Gates from photos by Beecie Kupersmith.

Index

Time-Life Books Inc. offers a wide range of fine record-
ings, including a *Rock 'n' Roll Era* series. For subscription
information, call 1-800-445-TIME, or write TIME-LIFE MUSIC,
Time & Life Building, Chicago, Illinois 60611.